Continuum Research Methods Series

Analysing Media Texts

Continuum Research Methods Series

Series Editor: Richard Andrews

Patrick Costello: *Action Research*

Andrew Burn and David Parker: *Analysing Media Texts*

Ian Gregory: *Ethics in Research*

Richard Andrews: *Research Questions*

Jill Jameson and Yvonne Hillier: *Researching Post-Compulsory Education*

Carole Torgerson: *Systematic Reviews*

Lia Litosseliti: *Using Focus Groups in Research*

Real World Research Series

Series Editor: Bill Gillham

Bill Gillham: *Case Study in Research Methods*

Bill Gillham: *Developing a Questionnaire*

Bill Gillham: *The Research Interview*

Analysing Media Texts

Andrew Burn and David Parker

continuum
LONDON • NEW YORK

Continuum

The Tower Building   15 East 26th Street
11 York Road   New York
London SE1 7NX   NY 10010

www.continuumbooks.com

British Library Cataloguing-in-Publication Data
A catalogue record for this book is available from the British Library.

ISBN: 08264 6470 X (paperback)

Typeset by RefineCatch Limited, Bungay, Suffolk
Printed and bound in Great Britain by MPG Books Ltd

To
Jenny and Dushani

Contents

Series Editor's Introduction

The Continuum Research Methods series aims to provide undergraduate, Masters and research students with accessible and authoritative guides to particular aspects of research methodology. Each title looks specifically at one topic and gives it in-depth treatment, very much in the tradition of the Rediguide series of the 1960s and 1970s.

Such an approach allows students to choose the books that are most appropriate to their own projects, whether they are working on a short dissertation, a medium-length work (15-40,000 words) or a fully-fledged thesis at MPhil or PhD level. Each title includes examples of students' work, clear explication of the principles and practices involved, and summaries of how best to check that your research is on course.

In due course, individual titles will be combined into larger books and, subsequently, into encyclopaedic works for reference.

The series will also be of use to researchers designing funded projects, and to supervisors who wish to recommend in-depth help to their research students.

Richard Andrews

Acknowledgements

We would like to thank our colleagues for their support, in particular Richard Andrews, Cary Bazalgette, David Buckingham, Diane Carr, Anton Franks, Carey Jewitt, Gunther Kress, Mark Reid and Brian Street.

1

Multimodality and Textual Analysis

The approach to the analysis of texts offered in this book will be a semiotic approach. To analyse a text made of words, you need some idea of how language works. Semiotics is based on the idea that similar understandings can be developed for systems of communication other than language. This is a relatively familiar idea with screen-based media and with visual design – we often talk in a general way about 'visual language' or 'the language of film', and these are perceptions of visual and audiovisual semiotics that have filtered through into the popular consciousness from decades of work on how such media make meaning.

Though what we recognize as a 'media text' still includes, importantly, film and television, it is subject to the same processes of rapid change which all kinds of text are experiencing in the age of digital media. We need to develop forms of semiotic analysis which recognize the particular properties of digital media texts such as web sites and computer games. We need to explore how such texts are quite different in some ways from their pre-digital predecessors; but also how they represent certain kinds of continuity.

Semiotics has a long history, and has been employed in many of its various forms by Media Studies. The version we will present here departs from earlier models in many ways, offering solutions to some of the difficulties which have beset semiotics in the past.

1

One such problem historically has been that semiotics developed into increasingly obscure variations, influenced by the range of theories collectively known today as 'post-structuralist'. These, along with postmodernist accounts of representation and communication, have often made it difficult to go about the business of analysing a text without becoming involved in strategic philosophical refusals to see meaning as logically determined in any way. While these theories valuably challenged the idea that meaning resides in fixed codes, representing fixed identities and a stable world, they also lost some of the clarificatory benefits of structuralist thought. We believe, as we shall show, that it is possible to recover this clarificatory purpose without losing the benefits of more recent developments in textual theory.

A second problem for semiotics (though also a set of productive developments) was the rise of Cultural Studies. This discipline, while it employed some semiotic perspectives, was in effect an assault on the abstraction of methods of textual analysis (especially those typical of late-seventies film theory) which saw viewers of the media as idealized spectators, rather than researching the behaviour of actual viewers. Cultural Studies represented a radical shift in emphasis, then, from text to audience. It used approaches derived from sociology and ethnography to research how real people engaged with film, television, romantic fiction, dance and popular music. Again, while the new territory revolutionized our idea of how ordinary people lived their cultural lives, it contributed less to textual analysis as such, seeing meaning-making more as part of the audience's interpretive effort than as part of the text's structural function. We believe that there is a balance to be restored here.

Andrew Tudor (1999) represents the current imbalance on Cultural and Media Studies in terms of a familiar opposition in sociology – the polar terms of structure and agency. Broadly speaking, he describes a move from an emphasis on the ability of structures (of language, ideology, text, the psyche) to determine the lives of people, to the reverse: an emphasis on the agency of people in determining their own meanings, pleasures, identities. He sees this opposition as sterile, arguing the need to find a new balance between structure and agency, and a sense of how the two are interdependent rather than opposed. In many ways, this book is an attempt to find practical solutions to the problem Tudor identifies.

A final aspect of media, film and cultural theory which should be briefly mentioned is a tradition of research in the political economy of the media. Such approaches allow for the study of how media texts are produced and consumed, looking at the significance of political and economic contexts and motivations. This makes it possible to explore issues of policy, regulation, globalization and patterns of consumption, as well as integrating these with more finely-focused case studies of audience groups

What does this amount to for students of the media today?

The legacy of these histories, we believe, makes it easier to study how media texts are produced and consumed than to study the texts themselves – or how the making of meaning is something that happens in a complex series of interactions between producer, text and reader.

In this book, therefore, we want to explore and develop theoretical approaches which look both at what a text is saying and how it is saying it, in a relatively clear and systematic way; while at the same time considering how real audiences engage with texts, and how texts are actually produced in the real world.

In our view, a theory enabling students to analyse media texts with some degree of confidence would need three things:

- A systematic approach to signification – to how texts make meanings, and how these meanings may be carried by a variety of different communicative forms, such as language, image, sound, gesture.

3

- The capacity to integrate textual analysis with an analysis of audiences and their engagement with the texts under scrutiny.
- The capacity to integrate textual analysis with the political, economic and social contexts in which texts are produced.

The approach which we will describe and model in this book has these capacities, and will provide students of the media with an analytical framework applicable not only to media texts, but, in principle, to any text of any kind. It is an approach rooted in social semiotics; and, more specifically, in a theory of multimodality.

What is multimodality theory?

Multimodality theory is a form of semiotics: a theory for the analysis of sign systems, or modes of communication. Its aim is to understand how we communicate with each other in many different ways, some of them mediated through the human body, such as speech, gesture or dance; others mediated by various technologies, such as writing, visual design, film, the internet and so on. It looks for semiotic principles common to all forms of communication that are relevant in any given instance (for example, if we are analysing a film, to consider how patterns of editing, spoken language and music might all contribute to the overall effect which we recognize as rhythm). And it looks for ways to describe systematically how these modes relate to each other: how the meaning of words might be changed by accompanying gestures; how images of outer space are changed by their combination with a Strauss waltz in Kubrick's *2001: A Space Odyssey*.

A social theory of communication

Multimodality is rooted in *social semiotics* (Hodge and Kress, 1988), a theory of sign-making which sees all acts of communication as social. In this theory, the sign-maker always has a social interest, or motivation, to communicate. It may be driven by the need to represent something in the world, whether this be an event, a belief, or the sign-maker themself. Or it may be driven by the need to establish relations with other people. In practice, whatever the emphasis, it will always perfom these two basic functions. However, our communications are dependent upon not only the semiotic resources available, whether these be paintbrushes, words or binary code, but also upon the social and cultural contexts in which we communicate. Analyses of the semiotic structures of texts produced for and by children and young people must, therefore, try to relate the analysis to these contexts, to determine what interests motivate the communications under scrutiny.

The social contexts of the media of contemporary communication have been extensively explored in the Cultural Studies research tradition. Of particular interest to educational researchers are studies by David Buckingham and colleagues of children, education and the media (Buckingham and Sefton-Green, 1994), of child audiences (Buckingham, 1996), of children's engagement with screen media (Buckingham, 2002) and of children's production of media texts (Buckingham *et al.*, 1995). In these studies, the motivation of children to engage with media texts to explore their world, their developing identities, their social allegiances, their tastes and pleasures, are documented and analysed. The picture which emerges is in many ways an optimistic one, where children's use of communicative forms is often knowledgeable, confident and purposeful. At the same time, a need is perceived for broad pedagogies – ways for children to learn how to understand and create media texts; though these forms of learning will not necessarily be located in formal educational contexts.

A functional theory

Multimodal theory sees all communicative acts as having three over-arching social functions. The first of these is **representational** – to represent some aspect of the world. The second is **orientational** – to establish relations between those who are communicating (whether these are real people and real relationships, as in a conversation, or between fictional characters and their real readers or viewers). The third function is **organizational** – to organize the communication as text, compose it in such a way that it is coherent and cohesive, so that it has conceptual unity and structural unity, both of which are necessary if the first two functions are to be fulfilled. (It should be noted that different writers have used different terms for these functions; ours are derived mostly from Lemke, 2002.)

These three functions provide a basis for the way we might approach analysis and the questions we might want to ask about a text, and we will return to them frequently as we tackle specific texts in the following chapters.

Communicative strata

Kress and van Leeuwen (2001) make a suggestion which has radical effects for textual analysts. They propose that texts, rather than being 'once-for-all' systems of signification, are in fact part of a dynamic set of processes of production, interpretation, reproduction and so on. To systematize this idea, they suggest four strata:

Discourse: which they define as 'knowledge of (some aspect of) reality'. We can see discourses as related to genres, so that human knowledge of some aspect of reality, whether large and grand (such as warfare or the Gothic imagination) or small and domestic (such as domestic chores or homework), will always be coded in particular communicative patterns. We see discourse not just as the precursor to any act of meaning-making (though it is always that), but also as a pervasive medium which completely surrounds it: all aspects of the making of a text are discursively situated and informed. Kress and van Leeuwen go on to point out that the interpretation of a text, itself an act of production in its own right, may take place in a different discursive context than that in which the text was produced, making for subversive counter-readings.

Design: design is the choice of mode. To tell a story, you need to decide whether it will be told orally, or in writing, or perhaps as a visual narrative. Richard Lanham has called this 'The Middlesex Question': a student approached him after a lecture at Middlesex University, saying that, as a designer, he was constantly having to decide whether to convey a message in image, text, speech or some other mode; and wanting to know on what he could base his decisions (Lanham, 2001). These decisions will produce particular sets of *affordances* – what each mode can offer, or indeed, what limitations it has. Language can tell a story whereas pictures can show it. A spoken story will be told in a specific time, and will make important use of intonation; a written story will be read in the reader's time, and intonation will be replaced by other devices. These are important differences.

Production: production involves the choice of medium. Modes are always realized through material media – once we have decided to tell a story, we have to decide whose voice will tell it; if we write it, we have to decide on the material tools for the writing (fountain pen or wordprocessor), the paper on which it will be printed, and so on. These choices, for multimodality, are not insignificant afterthoughts, but part of what makes the text mean what it does, and can affect the process of textual production significantly. The introduction of electronic media goes much further, not simply adding another set of material resources, but changing the nature of representation in profound ways. Digital media do not simply provide a different surface 'look' or aesthetic (Sinker, 2000), but offer ways to re-design elements of text already designed in a previous process (scanned images, edited text, edited video footage, multimedia ensembles). Furthermore, they provide new physical environments, tools and cultures within which communicative acts take place.

Distribution: texts can be distributed in many ways, but the ones we will focus on in this book are distributed through complex technologies, which can reproduce, disseminate, re-design, and transform in many different ways. This is partly to do with the nature of digital media, which are 'descended', in their social function, from earlier technologies of recording and transmission. In many ways, this function is still clearly discernible: television broadcasting systems and cinema projection systems deliver the moving image to its audiences; while the internet delivers webpages to its audiences. However, the plasticity of these media in the digital era means that the dividing line between the design and production of a text and its distribution becomes hard to distinguish. In the case of the internet, for instance, the medium of distribution is also, in many ways, the medium of design and production; and the webpage, once accessed by a reader, can be decomposed into text and image, or back into HTML, to become a resource for the production of new texts or for transformations based on the old one.

Why is multimodality of interest in education and social science research?

Firstly, an increase in multimodal communication can be seen in contemporary media. Obvious examples are print publications: newspapers, magazines and text-books all include many more visual images than was the case in the mid-twentieth century. The twentieth century also saw the introduction of new forms of multimodal text, especially the combinations of sound and image in cinema and television. The early twenty-first century is seeing new transformations and combinations of communicative modes in the internet, the rapidly-changing and extending functions of mobile devices, the convergent screen-based technologies, and the combinatorial possibilities of new digital formats for still image, moving image and sound. Interestingly, the word 'multimodality' is currently being used in the computing and telecommunications industries to refer to the way in which devices are moving away from a specialism in one mode to the use of several – so that your mobile phone will not only be for speaking and listening, but will take and receive pictures, enable text, show moving images, and access the internet.

The implication for textual analysts in the social sciences is twofold. As with any text, we need some way to analyse the processes and regimes of textual production: how is a computer game, for instance, authored? Stephen Poole (2000) describes how, in the early days of computer games, there was a kind of auteur period, where lone enthusiasts programmed entire games alone, and thus could be credited with a form of authorial responsibility for the 'game-text'. Now, he points out, games studios employ designers, script-writers, artists, animators, composers, programmers and directors – the authorship of the game is a highly-differentiated process involving many specialisms, more like the traditional division of labour involved in studio film-making. Schools can, and do, offer both of these polarized models. Students in schools can now make their own movies, combining music, sound, speech, graphics and the moving image all on one computer operated by one student; or they can simulate an industrial studio, with specialized divisions of labour undertaken by students working as a group. Multimodality offers ways to recognize the particular forms of meaning contributed by these different configurations of people and technologies in the making of a text.

Secondly, we need ways to analyse how texts are engaged

with by those who use them, read them, watch them, interpret them and interact with them. In educational research, this is a perennial concern, and one beset by changing and competing definitions of literacy and communication. As the multimodal nature of high-technology societies grows, these societies will reassess what communicative competences are needed by their citizens and how these are to be acquired and judged. The twentieth century saw a growth in Higher Education courses in the new media of film and television; and more recently in the even more new technologies of computer-based communication. The first undergraduate and postgraduate courses in computer games are appearing at the start of the twenty-first century. It seems certain that a move away from writing to what Walter Ong calls a 'secondary orality' is already offered by the digitally mediated spoken word, in speech recognition and synthesis, and in hybrid forms which combine features of writing and speech, such as text-messaging and chatroom communication (Ong, 2002).

More specifically for education researchers, debates about literacy learning in schools have widened in recent years. While in many Anglophone countries there is still a focus in policy and practice on word and sentence level print literacy, especially in the context of early years learning, educators are also asking: what might visual literacy look like (Raney, 1997), or how might moving image literacy be conceived (Burn and Parker, 2001)? Others are asking: what specific relations might there be between print literacy and the moving image (Parker, 1999); or between print literacy and computer games (Beavis, 2001)? More broadly still, the notions of multiliteracies and digital literacies suggest wider notions of communicative engagement across modes and media (Bigum *et al.*, 1997). Though this book will not directly address these debates, we hope to provide some frameworks for the analysis of texts which children engage with or make in the context of these expanding conceptions of literacy. We will return briefly to the question of literacy in the concluding chapter.

The researcher's focus

Multimodality is an emergent theory, and our version of it is different from those of other writers. It is important to be flexible and adaptive. Furthermore, this is a very brief introduction to multimodal analysis, and can only give a limited number of exemplar analyses. For more complete accounts, readers should see in particular:

- Kress and van Leeuwen (2001), for a general theory of multimodality;
- Hodge and Kress (1988), for a general theory of social semiotics;
- Kress and van Leeuwen (1996), for a social semiotic theory of visual design; and
- Jewitt and Kress (2003), for an edited book of different educational perspectives on multimodal literacies.

It is also important, as in any research, to define what it is that you are looking for – to ask a specific research question. In educational research, questions about multimodal texts may be related to many possible themes: what a text offers its readers; how it may be interpreted by them (and what might obstruct effective interpretation); what cultural uses it might be put to by children, parents, teachers, national policy-makers and curriculum designers; how children might design and produce their own multimodal texts; and what resources and technologies are available.

The method of this book will be to demonstrate how multimodal texts can be analysed using the frameworks outlined in this introduction. There are many possibilities here but we can only represent a sample of them. Most of our choices will be about whether we are focusing on one of the functions or more; one mode or more; and on one of Kress and van Leeuwen's strata or more. In Chapter 5, we will think beyond the text, to explore how readers interpret texts, and how this semiotic process is related to the semiotic structures of the text they are interpreting.

Finally, our choice of texts is necessarily arbitrary. It represents something of our own specialist interest in media education, within which websites, horror films, computer games and documentary videos are all legitimate objects of study as well as potential outcomes of students' own production work.

2

The Skater and the Old Man: Multimodal Design and Moving Image Production

In this chapter, we will look at the moving image. Its multimodal nature has been recognized in many different ways throughout the history of film theory. The theorist Christian Metz, who wanted to propose a way to analyse film as a language, decided that he would have to identify what aspects of film properly constituted this 'language', and chose some elements of the practices of filming and editing, calling these the 'cinematic'. The other modes that go to make up film – dramatic action, music and so on – he excluded from his analysis, calling these the 'filmic' (Metz, 1974). Our approach will combine these two, in what we have called the *kineikonic mode* – literally, the mode of the moving image (Burn and Parker, 2001; 2003).

We will analyse part of a short video made by three GCSE students in the UK, and will concentrate on the function of *representation*. Our analysis of the video will ask: how do pre-planned and improvized aspects of design and production shape the kinds of representation made by the filmmakers?

Skateboarding documentary video: discourse

The film was made in 2000 by a group of three GCSE Media Studies students (fifteen and sixteen years old) who attended a media arts college in Cambridge, UK. Their task was to create their own documentary, and within that form to make something that reflected the specific characteristics of the 'tribute' video genre. An example of this genre (a video about the Manchester United footballer Eric Cantona) was shown at school and was critically analysed before filming began.

The students' film runs for approximately five minutes and takes 'skateboarding' as its subject matter. It situates itself within a quite specific genre – the documentary – and it functions within that genre in a number of interesting ways. In one sense it is speaking directly to skateboarders, or to 'youth' generally, and the discourse which this orientation invokes informs the content of the film, the music, and the close attention to particular skateboarding moves or tricks. However, a second discourse is operating which links the filmmakers to the audience of their teachers and examiners, a discourse that is driven by the need to show, through practical production, an understanding of the genre and its conventions, with the ultimate aim of gaining accreditation towards a public examination.

Design and production

We will analyse one section from the video, taken from approximately midway through the film (Figure 1). In this sequence the conception of the authoritarian adult world is represented by an elderly man who attempts to move the skateboarders away from the precinct outside an office complex where he works. We want to look in some detail at the mixture of gesture, speech, sound, action, music and words, and to consider how this multimodal ensemble is shaped through decisions made during the processes of filming and editing.

To begin with, the boys making the film have a planned set of representational resources, integrated by the logic of the kineikonic mode, and designed using specific conventions of the tribute video they have studied. They have an idea of what kinds of shots they want, noted down as a shot list. These shots

Figure 1   Six screengrabs from the skateboarding video.

aim to construct the subjects of their documentary as skateboarding heroes. They have also been asked to include an interview sequence; they plan to interview one of the skateboarders, one of his friends and a number of passers-by.

Secondly, they have two skateboarders, members of their own year group at school. In one sense, these are the subjects of the documentary – to be represented; in another sense, they are the material substance of the representation – they are, as it were, acting themselves. This will happen in a consciously designed way: they will be directed by the filmmakers, rather than being filmed in the so-called 'fly-on-the-wall' manner.

As we shall see, however, they are also collaborators in the design and production processes, in ways not necessarily anticipated by the filmmakers.

Thirdly, they have the camera, and those aspects of the kineikonic it affords – framing, shot distance, camera angle, focus, light control and camera movement.

Fourthly, they have the editing process, and use a Media 100 digital editing workstation. Here, they have the final combinatorial affordances of kineikonic production, such as the assembly and trimming of shots, the construction of transitions, the articulation of the soundtracks.

So far, these modes and media are familiar, and suggest an orderly, conventional view of how design and production works in the moving image: scenes are planned, filmed and edited, and representational resources are gathered, synthesized and assembled.

However, nothing in the real world is as neat as this. The analysis should take in the typical raggedness and improvisation that is part of any creative enterprise, any effort of communication. In the case of this film, this improvisation was always a part of the work. As well as planning shots, the young filmmakers were always on the lookout for serendipitous moments to capture which would fit the discourse of a rebellious subculture they wanted to represent. We will see this improvisation as a form of dramatic process.

Dramatic design

During the filming of the skateboard set-pieces, outside a university building in the city where they were filming, an unexpected event occurred. An irritable man emerged from the building, and tried to send the skateboarders away. This episode was clearly a routine part of the lives of skateboarders, whose choice of locations for the best skating often leads to territorial and generational conflict.

We can view such events as a kind of social drama, in which both parties in the conflict are playing out their chosen social roles. Erving Goffman's theory of the dramatization of social selves (1959) offers a framework for the analysis of such real life drama. These roles, he makes clear, are constructed selves, put together for public display, in contrast to the hidden selves we allow to appear in the 'backstage' areas of our lives, especially in our homes. In our film, then, the clash between the skate-boarders and the old man assumes a kind of ritual quality. There is a heightening of dramatic display, exemplified in the old man's exaggerated gestures shooing the boys away, and in the antagonistic tone and words of one of the skaters, who says: 'I don't speak English.'

However, when we consider that, at this moment, a film is being made about the skateboarders, it becomes clear that the processes of representation through dramatic action are work-ing as a series of layers of kinds of role-play with quite different *modalities*, or truth-claims (see Chapter 4 for a fuller account of modality).

Firstly, there are the skaters, who, though going through their usual routines, are performing these for the camera, and so presenting a kind of dramatic display which has a different kind of status. It is produced as a conscious representation, and includes processes which can be seen as a kind of proto-editing, as the boys break off a trick, repeat it, do it to order, in the kinds of disjunctive articulation typical of moving image production. This is a kind of drama; but its disjunctiveness is a design for the moving image, not for the usual display of the skaters in 'real' life, nor for the theatre, in both of which continuity is the rule.

As far as this process is concerned, we can see the filmmakers and the skateboarders as collaborators in the design of the film. The skaters deploy physical action, the informal choreography of skateboarding, and the performance of a subcultural role complete with costume, gestural and spoken repertoires and attitude! The filmmakers deploy the tools of the moving image.

17

The semiotic principles informing the whole process are those of the kineikonic mode, so that all movements, gestures and speech are modelled by the framing, angle and movement of the camera, and the intentionality of the envisaged edit.

Secondly, the moment the old man enters the scene, the role-play of the skaters changes. Instead of a performed re-enactment of their routines, they move towards the kind of improvised role-play which is real life, as Goffman describes it. The battle with the old man is a real battle; the dramatized documentary becomes real life. However, the boys still know they are being filmed. This drama, then, has a double onto-logical status – it is being played out as real life performance, and as mediated performance for the camera.

Thirdly, the old man does not know he is being filmed. For him, then, the event has the status of life, unmediated by any representational process other than the first level of representa-tion involved in the 'presentation of self in everyday life', as Goffman puts it.

Before analysing the text of this sequence, we need finally to consider the representational work of the filmmakers at the point the old man enters their film. At this point, then, there is a change in the process of design. Up to that point, they have had control of all the variables of the kinekonic mode – the dra-matic presentation of the skateboarders, the choice of location, the framing of shots and the movement of the camera. At the point of the old man's entrance, not only does the ontological status of the dramatic representation gain another layer, but also the process of kineikonic design changes. Again, drama offers good analogies. Before the old man's entrance, the film-ing is like a scripted drama, carrying out pre-designed semiotic moves. After the entrance, it becomes like improvised drama. New representational material arrives as the life-drama is played out. A new temporality comes into play, the continuous realtime of everyday performance, so the filming can no longer operate as proto-editing, capturing disjunctive frag-ments independently of the temporal sequence and duration of real life events. Nor do they have complete control over framing and shot distance. We will consider, in our analysis, how this improvisatory, realtime camera design, the characteristic mode of documentary film based on actual events, is combined with editing, and with the footage from the pre-planned sequences.

At the same time, we must consider how the *representational function* of this sequence is changed by the arrival of the old man. In effect, this is a narrative sequence, but the original plan for the tribute video is a particular kind of narrative: that of an actor who demonstrates his skills. In terms of what in language would be called transitivity, this is a grammatical sequence which is intransitive – the actor acts; but not upon any object or goal. This is a hero without a villain. At the moment of the old man's arrival, the narrative changes from the intransitive tribute structure to a transitive structure – the villain arrives; his actions are directed at the skateboarders, while he in turn becomes the goal of their trespass and rebellious language.

Leo and the old man: the kineikonic and its subsidiary modes

We will consider the impact each mode has in the articulation of the sequence described above by considering the relationship between mode and meaning. To do this we will first look at each mode in turn, then move on to look at the way they are integrated by the kineikonic mode through the interplay of shots, their design and order and their relationship with one another in space and through time.

Music: the contextual metaphor

At the beginning of this sequence the fast tempo and insistent rhythm of thrash metal music sets up a clear opposition between the filmmakers and the establishment values they are about to contest during the exchange between the old man and Leo. The music functions here to amplify the representation of the skateboarders as heroes, and to set up a cultural reference point for an insider audience – clearly the choice of music reflects the kinds of tastes and preferences of skateboarders and thereby suggests a value position. The music is edgy, aggressive – the lyrics spell out the kind of disenfranchised perspective taken by outsiders in relation to a perceived mainstream set of values. Finally, it acts as a rhythmic determinant: many of the shots are cut on the 4/4 beat, so that the music track functions as 'initiating rhythm' (van Leeuwen, 1985). Here, an aspect of the organizational structure of the text across two subsidiary modes of the kineikonic (image and music) functions to support the text's representation of the skaters and its orientation to its audience.

Action: determining agency

The actions of Leo and the old man are framed in a way that clearly defines our understanding of agency in this sequence. Leo is invested with the characteristics of 'hero' through the use of the skateboard and the appropriation of the public space outside the office building. He performs a series of jumps using the skateboard, involving actions that require timing, speed and co-ordination. The camera describes a space for him to move through, then pans with him to reinforce our sense of identification with his actions and his right to left, foreground to background trajectory. His actions on the arrival of the old man are to stop the tricks, and begin a territorial circling of the precinct. As we have seen, this initiates an ontologically different kind of dramatic action, in which the pre-designed performative segments give way to a continuous display of antagonism at real-life level; while the intransitive actions of the tricks are succeeded by the transitive act of territorial appropriation, with the old man as goal.

Shot level: the signification of order

There are four shots spliced together to make up this sequence. Firstly, the skateboard trick shot. Secondly, the pan across, right to left, as Leo skates across the precinct. Thirdly, a medium longshot of the old man's reactions. Fourthly, a response shot, Leo 'talking back' to the old man. What is interesting about the arrangement of these shots is the way in which their position relative to one another suggests the dynamic nature of the argument between the two protagonists. A clear example of this is the way the old man's gesture of exasperation – used as the cue for the on-screen title 'old man gives up' – is actually taken from an earlier series of events. The fact that it is positioned later in the narrative sequence – removed from its 'real-time' position – shows the extent to which the editing process creates different articulations of the spatial and temporal elements of the film footage to alter the meaning; in this case, to intensify the meanings already expressed in the sequence.

Written language

The use of titling here has a practical, intermodal purpose. Because the boy operating the camera is unable to get close to the old man, and is having to improvise from the position he happens to be in, the old man is further away than is ideal. The arrival of the villain of the piece, if this were pre-planned, would probably be shown in close-up. We can tell that the cameraman wants to achieve this effect, as he zooms in on the old man when he realizes what is happening. The zoom on the camcorder only takes him to a medium longshot, however. The boys solve the problem that the old man is not represented in the foreground by using the title 'Enter Old Man' (and later 'Old Man Gives Up'). The writing lends the necessary salience, names the villain, contributes the alarming properties of the colour red to the visual design of the piece, and amplifies the dramatic status of this actor.

Speech: the accentuation of agency

There is only one moment where speech features in this sequence. During the confrontation between the old man and Leo the music fades out just enough for the words 'I don't speak English' to be heard. This sarcastic remark by Leo, his rejoinder to the man's protests, serves to accentuate his role in relation to 'established order' – he is the heroic actor, the old man the villainous goal of his remark. In common parlance, Leo has the last word. Again, this is both 'designed' by Leo as part of the real-life improvisation of the event, and re-designed in intensified form as an element on the soundtrack by the editors.

Movement over time: compression and repetition

We have already mentioned the fact that events are re-ordered in this sequence in order to emphasize a particular meaning. The management of time through the editing process allows for easy reconfiguration of order, or of a number of alternative orders, all of which could be saved digitally and compared. Key moments can be slowed to accentuate their importance. Trick shots in the early sequences are accorded high value by being repeated and/or slowed during the editing process. Superfluous material, or moments which threaten to disrupt the narrative or create ambiguity in relation to the key protagonists can be easily excised. In this sequence we can clearly discern the fact that of the four shots set up, none appear to be used comprehensively. Each one has been trimmed or altered in some way to simultaneously keep the pace of the narrative high and the meaning clear. As we have seen, however, this disjunction of real-time events to create new meanings happens both in filming and editing for the pre-planned sequences; but only during editing in the improvised sequence, since the camera is caught up in the real-time events.

Designing social space

The spaces occupied by people and objects in this sequence are also significant. An example of movement through space that enhances the opposition between protagonist and antagonist is the freedom of movement accorded to Leo and the fixed, confined presence of the old man. Similarly, we, as spectators, are spatially much closer to Leo than we are to the old man until, crucially, the old man admits 'defeat', at which point we are taken closer to him than we have been before. This makes a virtue of necessity – the cameraman is really further from the old man than he is from Leo. However, since the social reason for this in real life – the enmity between the boys and the man – is identical with the relationship the filmmakers wish to represent, the physical distance serves as an appropriate signifier of social distance. The only problem remaining is that a closer shot is required to accord appropriate villainous status to the old man – a problem solved, as we have suggested above, by the use of titling.

Pulling the modes together

These elements are blended through the editing process, which we can imagine as a kind of multimodal mixing-desk. Its function is not simply that of assembly, but of re-design. Different editing software packages will adopt variations on a basic interface design, but the principles remain similar. There is a viewing window where each clip can be viewed. An edit bar where clips can be moved along a time line and set against other elements, also time-based, such as music and sound effects. There is also a 'shelf' or 'bin' where imported clips can be stored as visual icons before being viewed in the main window. When clips are dragged into the time-line it is possible to extract the audio from each clip and, if necessary, to replace it with another audio source. In essence, the editing software represents a mechanism for viewing the modes separately in

23

disaggregated form, for provisonally joining them to experiment with combinatorial effect, and for altering scalar values such as brightness or colour saturation, speed, volume, and so on.

The interplay of shots that make up the exchange between Leo and the old man suggest a purposeful remix of modal properties through the governing mode (the kineikonic) which orchestrates the whole message. How does this happen and what are the traces of the remixing process we might look for in the finished moving image production?

We suggest that there are three important principles of multimodal combination at work in this piece.

Firstly, there are what Metz (1974) called the *pre-filmic*. Properly speaking, these are 'found' semiotic material, which are made in modes which do not refer to the kineikonic. In the case of this film, there are two obvious examples – the music and the social performance of the old man. Neither of these has been made with film in mind; both are appropriated by the makers to signifiy elements of the cultural values invested in the film.

Secondly, there are what we will call *pro-filmic* resources. These are modal assemblies made for the kineikonic. Here, the obvious example is the skateboarders. They assemble a performed version of their cultural selves using the movements, rhythm, costume, gesture and speech of skateboarding; but articulated within the kineikonic mode, already shaped by its organizing structures.

Thirdly, there are the framing, assembly and value-scaling modes of the camera and edit suite, that element of the kineikonic in which Metz found the *cinematic* language. Here, the signifiying properties of camera frame, distance, movement, angle, and edit suite assembly and rescaling of digital strips of moving image and sound are deployed by the filmmakers.

Finally, there is the question of how the modes combine, raising two important questions which we have referred to in the introduction to this book. One is the question of *functional load* – which mode has a stronger weight, or a determining function, at any given moment? The second is: how do the modes impact on each other?

For these last two questions, we will refer to two examples. Firstly, the combination of music and speech in the sound-track. It is clear that, throughout this episode, music is given the dominant position through volume – any speech of the old man is literally drowned out. That this is a signifier of the power attributed to the skaters by the filmmakers is evident when the intermodal weighting is reversed, at the point where Leo makes his sarcastic rejoinder. Here, then, the relation between the modes is one of *opposition* (the music against the old man's speech) and *complementary* (the music and Leo's speech).

The second example is the filming of the skating tricks. The four modes in play are the choreographed movements of Leo, the camera's construction of the shot, using a zoomed close-up and a movement which follows the movement of the skater; the music; and the editing of the shot, which is determined by the rhythm and length of the skateboard moves and by the rhythm of the music. These modes are all in a *complementary* relation, working to produce a common rhythm, a common cultural discourse and a narrative placement of the skater at the centre of a sequence. It is hard to say that any of these modes carries a greater weight – they seem balanced in their weighting.

The final example is the use of titling to aggrandize the old man. As we have seen, this is a *compensatory* use of one mode to accomplish what cannot be done in another, in this instance, to raise the salience of the old man in a shot which had to be further away than was ideal. In this case, the red letters have a particular salience – they have an initiating function, leading us into the desired viewing of the sequence.

Conclusion

A combination of two kinds of analysis here – of the processes of design and production, and of the finished text itself – reveals a good deal about the way in which this text functions to represent an idea, a culture and a group of people. It shows that the process of filmmaking depends on how the filmmakers construct a representation in the kineikonic mode through the disjunctive narrative of the moving image, through the importation of musical rhythm and style, and through a witty and stylish combination of dramatic event, text, speech and location. But it also demonstrates how making the moving image is itself a kind of drama, where the burden of representation shifts between participants in the process of making the film. It shows something of how the material bodies and movements of the actors oscillate between the real-time drama of everyday life and performance for the camera; and how the filmmakers themselves are caught up in this social drama, as partial observers, and as improvisatory re-makers, carving out a new version of the event.

Methodological points

1. Because the moving image is such an extended process of design and production, it can be valuable to take a diachronic view (across time) of this process. In this case, the succession of modes and media used – how they come into play, what they are useful for and who deploys them – can all be studied.
2. This analysis focuses on the function of *representation* – how particular ideas and narratives are constructed. A different analysis might focus on the *orientational* function – how this text addresses its two different audiences of peers and examiners.
3. The notion of drama as a mode is tentatively used here.

Clearly, the moving image subsumes drama, itself a complex and powerful ensemble of modes, in certain ways. The history of the cinema is closely related to drama, using sets, actors, directors, scripts, lighting and so on in ways originally derived from and still closely related to theatre. On the other hand, as we have tried to show here, any representation of human beings in documentary style is likely to encounter other forms of dramatic performance, those which Goffman (1959) identifies as the processes by which we construct the public selves through which we live our lives. This is a complex area, and there remains much to be worked on.

4. There are important aspects of the kineikonic mode as a multimodal ensemble which we have only touched on here. One of these is rhythm, which, as Bordwell and Thompson (2001) remark, is not well understood. See van Leeuwen (1985 and 1999) for some thought-provoking ideas on this.

5. The data collected to inform analysis of the moving image can be varied. In this case, we have relied only on observations of the filming and editing process, and on the final texts.

   Other data to collect can be:

   - storyboards and other design materials
   - filmed processes of design and production
   - interviews with participants
   - screengrabs of editing software, especially the editing 'timeline'

6. In the analysis of moving image texts, it may be helpful, as we have done here, to use screengrabs to represent shots. However, it may also be important to note other aspects of the text, to show how, for instance, the image sequence, the editing structure, the vocal track and music are articulated. See van Leeuwen's article on rhythm in film (1985) for an example of how different modes can be tabulated.

3

Chocolate Politics: Analysing Websites

The question explored in this chapter is how two kinds of social interest motivate websites offering forms of 'e-learning' to children. We will begin by looking at the *organizational function* of the texts and what this organization allows their users to do; but will also consider how they present ideas, narratives and representations of their subject, as well as how they address their audience. We want to consider how the visual elements of design, written language, and the nodes and links of hypertext combine to offer multiple-user pathways. How do these structures represent the content areas central to the sites; how do they construct relations between text and audience? And, as we are focusing on educational websites, what kind of models of learning are produced by these sites?

The websites

The texts we will analyse are two UK websites which both represent chocolate companies and their products. One, the Dubble website, represents a new Fair Trade chocolate bar for children; the other, the Cadbury's Learning Zone, represents the Cadbury chocolate company. Both sites are centrally concerned with the representation of chocolate, and also of particular ethical messages related to the production of chocolate. Both are also educational sites, targeted at the children who, while self-evidently the audience of apparently disinterested educational processes, are also the target market for the chocolate which both sites are implicitly promoting. A necessary distinction here, however, is that the ethical message of Cadbury's is incidental to its commercial operation, while the ethical message of the Dubble site is intrinsic to the economic structure of the chocolate production.

In both cases, a specific cultural context and a set of discourses are discernible. In the case of the Dubble bar, the context is that of Fair Trade and the associated practices of ethical trading, and charitable or state-funded aid programmes for developing countries, in this case Ghana. The Dubble bar is promoted jointly by the UK aid charity Comic Relief and by the Fair Trade chocolate company the Day Chocolate Company, a third of which is owned by the Ghanaian cocoa-farmers' co-operative, Kuapa Kokoo. The website is part of a project funded by the UK government's Department for International Development, intended to link children in schools in the UK with children in schools in Ghana. The website combines discourses of childhood, education, consumer advertising and aid.

The Cadbury's site is The Cadbury Learning Zone, an educational website affiliated to the DfES-funded Channel 4 Gridclub service, and listed as an approved site by the UK's National Grid for Learning (NGfL). It represents its own product and its own company, constructing a particular narrative of the history of chocolate production in a paternalistic Quaker tradition, rooted in an ethic of social reform of labour conditions, both within the company and beyond. Again, the site operates within discourses of childhood, education, advertising and chocolate.

These discourses involve highly-contested beliefs, value systems and political and economic practices. Chocolate, for instance, is a product which, through its manufacture and distribution, has recently been implicated in child slavery in western Africa, and extreme poverty among cocoa-producers as a result of low and unstable cocoa prices. It has also been linked with the growing crisis of food disorders and obesity in the developed world. The other major discourse shared by the sites, education, is similarly a highly-contested practice in the context of the internet, seen by governments as the ultimate delivery vehicle for online curricula which digitally replicate traditional transmission models of pedagogy; and by other sections of the educational and academic communities as opportunities for dynamic new forms of learning in which students can determine the patterns, routes and content of their learning more autonomously. Whether such optimism is justified in the case of these two examples is a question we will begin to ask.

Organization: the design of learning

For each website, we will analyse two types of textual organization, which we will call *static* (the relations between elements with no hypertextual links) and *dynamic* (relations between hyperlinked elements). Both are governed by principles of visual design at the level of any given screen; though in some ways the logic of spatial design is more prominent in the textual organization, while hypertextual relations occur in a more obviously temporal sequence. There is also a relation between the two – the salience of the dynamic elements is increased through visual rollover reference to a hypertextual depth.

An important aspect of these structures is how they offer routes through the experiences they provide. Jay Lemke (2002) distinguishes between two notions of text here – the *semiotic text*, or sequence of signs presented to the reader; and the *meaning-text*, which is the reader's interpreted movement through this sequence. In hypertext, Lemke argues, the semiotic text presents more or less explicit trajectories; while the interpretation of meaning by the reader proceeds as traversals. These notions are related to Kress and van Leeuwen's idea of *reading path* –

Figure 2 The Cadbury Learning Zone website.

that particularly in the context of visual design, there is a double structure in which the text offers implied routes around the design, while the reader engages with this to design their own reading (Kress and van Leeuwen, 1996).

The Cadbury's Learning Zone site (Figure 2) is designed so that salience is indicated by structures of centrality, both vertical and horizontal, by their size and by their static or dynamic status. The large central oval shape contains symbolic representations of the 'curriculum' offered by the site: Maths, History and Environment. This page offers links to each of the three areas. The group of cartoon children are positioned on the right of the image, so that if we read from left to right, they appear as objects of the curriculum. Unlike the abstract representations of the curriculum, the children are a static image, with no hypertextual depth. Though we may test them out with a rollover, they go nowhere, limiting their salience.

If we follow the Maths link we reach a choice of activities, though the fact that they are numbered suggests a strong trajectory. Text is central, both literally and in terms of its functional load. Maths problems are presented as written language, as in a traditional Maths textbook. The activity is nothing to do with chocolate production in reality, as the verbs in the instruction suggest: 'Count it out'; 'What to do'; 'Work out how many'. The numbers are meaningless, relating to no economic context, even of how much chocolate is produced and consumed in the UK in a day, a week, a month or a year, all of which contexts would suggest a range of possible reactions. Even more striking would be calculations of cocoa-farmers' annual incomes, say, compared to the revenue generated from the chocolate bars made from their annual harvest in Europe or America.

A print-centred curriculum is constructed. The action required of the child audience is simply an online version of that which a traditional Maths book of the 1950s might demand. The association with chocolate production is reduced heavily by the low modality of the cartoon images and the severance of any connection with factual information about the economics of chocolate production. ('Modality' is the text's way of signifying its truth-claim; see Chapter 4 for a fuller account.)

So far, we can say that there are relatively few links, that they indicate very strongly a hierarchical organization in which governing ideas break down into successively finer sub-categories until we reach (two screens further down) the activities. The coherence of this text – its conceptual unity – is an educational idea represented by the three themes in the learning zone, themselves a condensed representation of the UK National Curriculum. Any conceptual thread implied by the apparently active group of children embarking on a quest is abandoned, unsupported by the hypertextual structure.

The Dubble site designs learning differently (Figure 3). The reading path is much less obviously signalled. We are drawn to a 'welcome' message, centrally placed, so that successive choices might go either right or left. In terms of size, the image of the Ghanaian girl on the right is most salient. Like the Cadbury's site, then, the structure of the page suggests the agency of children. Here, however, the importance of the image signalled by its size is supported by its hypertextual

Figure 3 The Dubble website.

function, which links to a page giving further representations of the lives of cocoa-farmers and their children.

There is an interesting mixture of visual links on the homepage, with a total menu of thirty-one links arranged in three clusters on the page. This configuration offers a dense, multiply connected hypertextual network. Some of the links offer multimodal alternatives – that is, we can reach the same route via a text-based link or an image-based link. It is also multimodal in that it offers different types of experience employing different communicative forms – light-hearted role-play, including games, reading and watching movies. The coherence of this page is structured around the conceptual unity of the chocolate idea; its cohesion is the loose cohesion of the magazine, offering a variety of elements in a structure which relates highly specific and dense elements, most with the depth of a hypertext link, with an overall design which is deliberately vague, as if to say these are all interesting things to do – you choose your own way through them. This contrasts vividly with the Cadbury page, in which relatively imprecise elements (e.g. 'Maths', or the block of writing at the bottom of the page) are related to highly specific combinatorial structures, which effectively says here are some vague things to do; you should do them in this way.

Orientation: teaching and selling

Our main question about how these websites orientate themselves towards their audience is: What kind of communication is this? Education, for instance, broadly speaking, could be seen as a kind of offer of information, along with a kind of encouragement to take up the offer or, in more authoritarian contexts, an instruction or command. Other forms of education could be characterized by questions (the traditional Socratic mode), which lead the learner to discover answers. However, these two websites are not entirely disinterested educational resources (if there is such as thing). Both of them promote their product, though with different motivations. In this respect, we might expect them to deploy rhetorical structures typical of advertising. Advertising has a complex relation to what, in language, is the system of *mood*. Halliday saw this as performing two basic interpersonal functions: to make offers or to make demands (for the visual equivalents of demand and offer, see Kress and van Leeuwen, 1996). In one (original) sense, advertisements *offer* information about their product. In another sense, they *demand* that the audience purchase the product: either implicitly, by seduction, invitation, exhortation, suggestion; or through direct imperatives – the hard sell.

For instance, under the historical section, the Cadbury's site

35

offers information as images, from the Victorian past of the company; and each of these link to a text-box, which tells us something about the company's ethical practices. However, it also presents forms of instruction, particularly in its presentation of trajectories. In the Maths section, for instance, the activities related to chocolate production are listed numerically, as if instructing readers to follow them in that sequence.

Its verbal language employs the formal register of a traditional pedagogy, which implies a considerable social distance between the teacher and the student:

Nicola is in the packing department. It is time for lunch.

Or:

Working in a Victorian factory could be hard and unpleasant and sometimes very dangerous.

A particular relationship is also implied by the heavy use of written language in the Maths and History sections, as if to say that the print-mode is the one favoured by the educator, and the literacy of the learner must cope with this.

Where the Cadbury's site 'speaks' with a single 'voice', that of the invisible instructor, establishing an uninterrupted relation of didact to pupil, the Dubble site speaks with multiple voices. On the homepage, we saw that the image of the Ghanaian girl was juxtaposed with text reading: 'I'll think of you when you eat a Dubble bar, and when you eat it, think of me too!'

The voice of this message, though linked with a photographic image, functions like the form of address in a charity ad. The imperative form of the verb ('think of me'), linked with what Kress and van Leeuwen (1996) call a *demand image act*, in which the represented figure gazes directly at the viewer, functions to demand a serious ethical reflection by the chocolate consumer. The seriousness of the demand is modified, however, by the smiling face of the girl in the photograph, less typical of the charity ad genre.

There are other demands on the page, in the form of language imperatives: 'Check out the schools linking page'; 'Sign up as a Dubble Agent'; 'Watch Dubble movies'. The demand function here is modified again, by informal language and by the implied pleasurable nature of the activities, so that it is experienced as an invitation by virtue of its propositional content, in spite of its status as grammatical imperative.

The presentation of the Dubble bar implies various types of modified demand to buy the bar. These demands are, by contrast with the activities, never formally signalled as demands or imperatives, always as offers; though their propositional content reveals them as demand. For instance, the text-box linked with the image of the Ghanaian girl, saying: 'When you eat Dubble, think of me . . .' contains a formal imperative ('think of me') which is actually an invitation to exercise empathy; whereas the preceding clause, which is formally indicative, is a propositional demand in that it assumes the reader *will* eat Dubble.

Representation: chocolate and childhood

Both sites are centrally concerned to represent chocolate and childhood. As we have seen, the Dubble site combines the two themes in the the largest image on its home page, as well as in the text. As with all media which use combinations of mode, in this case visual design and written language, we can ask a question about *functional load* – what is it that the two modes are respectively doing? The visual design presents the photographic image of a Ghanaian child as an obvious entry point for the viewer of the site, its salience marked by the size of the image and the rotated position on the page, at odds with the straight construction of the other frames. The image, then, says that this child is the actor in this narrative of chocolate production – she is shown holding a basket of cocoa-pods.

The functional specialism of the writing is different. It plays to its strengths, representing internal processes of thought and feeling, where the image deals in the specificity of place and outward appearance.

Image and text have a complementary relationship; and orientationally, as we have seen, both point the same way – outwards at the reader. They indicate a dominant theme of the site, a reaching-out from the developing world to the developed world.

Childhood and chocolate are also represented on this page implicated as semiotically fused in the cartoon character located in the 'Dubble Agents' box. Though this image is smaller, it is given salience by its central position in the page, by its colour and by its incorporation of the Dubble logo. The image of an anthropomorphized cocoa bean in a secret agent hat and raincoat derives its cultural meaning from children's animations and from advertising strategies for chocolate and breakfast cereals, such as Coco-Pops, M&Ms and Frosties.

That the site is concerned with the promotion of the chocolate bar itself is also clear. The logo appears three times, serving as a possible reading path. It is also a cohesive device linking to punning transformations of 'doubleness' – double relationships between children in the UK and Ghana; 'Dubble Agents', inviting children to join in the promotion of the bar, and so on. The design of the lettering involves a semiotics of childhood familiar in print and broadcast media – uneven lettering signifying playfulness, red signifying activity and dynamism. The use of branding to convey a message of ethical trading here is a kind of semiotic use of the enemy's tools – a deployment of the semiotics of global capitalism in the service of a message opposed to the interests of the multinational corporatism which controls the vast bulk of chocolate production and retail.

Finally, the Dubble site presents a variety of narratives of chocolate production, which represent the agency of the cocoa-farmers strongly through the dominance of photographic image, quicktime movies and linking narrative writing. Here the site has the difficult task of presenting the plight of the farmers without representing them as helpless victims and recipients of aid handouts, which it addresses by making them the actors of the images and movies, and by representing them as cheerful and using full colour (contrasting with the black-and-white so typical of charity and campaign ads).

The Cadbury's site deploys many of the same strategies. Children are also represented through a visual discourse which associates them with cartoon figures; though here, the children themselves (only white children) are represented as cartoon figures. As we have seen, the initial appearance of agency in the images of the children is undermined by the lack of hypertextual depth and by their disappearance as we get down to the 'meat' of the curriculum – the language and number-based activities. Orientationally, this can be seen as a modality strategy, denoting the truth claim of the text. The cartoon figures of the Cadbury children, and those in the page which depicts the process of chocolate production, suggest a distance from reality.

In another page, showing the process of chocolate production, the cocoa-farms of West Africa are reduced to the brief, comic notation of cartoon cocoa-beans harvesting the cocoa crop (Figure 4). As in the Dubble site, the harvest is cheerful,

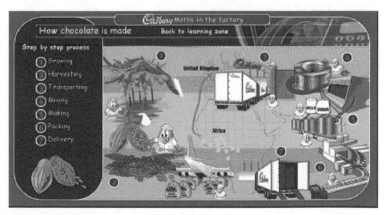

Figure 4   Cadbury's Learning Zone: chocolate production.

but here the cheerfulness conceals the economic reality rather than modifying its affective impact. This is the case partly because the unalloyed modality of the cartoon figures pushes the reality of cocoa-production into the background, and partly because the visual narrative is not amplified by any information about the economics of chocolate production. In the Dubble site, by contrast, the visual narrative has a modality of documentary proximity to real-world events, and is amplified by written information about the economic process of Fair Trade. So while cartoon cocoa-beans are also used, deploying a familiar 'child-friendly' discourse, the modality of the cartoon world is modified by its conjunction with photographic images and moving image sequences of children and cocoa-harvesting.

In fact, these few cartoon figures on one page are the only representation of Africa on the entire Cadbury site. The story of chocolate production elsewhere on the site is constructed historically as the story of Cadbury's, the company, which assembles archive photographs and written exposition to displace the political economy of the present-day production of cocoa in Africa by a narrative of past events in chocolate production in England. So the ethical concern becomes not one of how impoverished cocoa-farmers can get a fair deal for their product, but one of how Cadbury's stood up against the vicious practices of Victorian industry by treating their workers well.

Conclusion

The Cadbury's site in general, then, designs an educational process with marked characteristics. Representationally, it avoids images of the real world, except where they are distanced by time; and it avoids information which would open up the painful debates about the economics of chocolate production and their consequences for African farmers and children. Interactively, it reduces opportunities for learners to choose and design their own priorities, pathways and activities; and it offers activities associated with traditional models of pre-digital learning: print literacy with minimal visual interest; numerical problem-solving in a cultural vacuum; and passive reception of information. As hypertext, the site is designed hierarchically. It proposes a series of layers like the extension of classroom activities, ordered across the top by National Curriculum categories. There is some choice but the heavily flagged trajectory is to follow the activities in sequence. Should a child ever spend an extended period of time on this site, it is likely that the traversal of links and nodes would be very similar to the trajectory presented by the site.

The Dubble site is quite differently organized, deploying the affordances of web design to create a more user-directed learning experience. This design offers considerable openness – it balances the salience of its many nodes so that no one trajectory is implied, and many traversals are possible. Information about the core message of the site, the political economy of chocolate production and fair trade, and the need to connect lives in Ghana with lives in the UK, is presented multimodally, catering for a wide variety of learning styles typical of both formal and informal learning. The story of chocolate production is presented as a series of image and text designs resembling a board game. On the left, for those who prefer it, is text, presenting the information in traditional fashion. On the board game are images leading to stages of production, in turn offering snapshots of real people and their lives, a mini computer game related to the stage of production, and a streamed video of the process.

This curriculum looks quite different. It is not segmented by the categories of the National Curriculum. It suggests not an epistemology abstracted from contemporary life, but one closely implicated with the images, words, experiences and pleasures of children on two continents. Its map of learning is not structured by pre-determined sequences, but by loose multiple connections, offering the audience the chance to design their own reading path, their own multimodal assembly. A

41

reader can work here largely visually, reading still images of people, films of cocoa production, and playing the games; or largely textually, putting together chunks of written information into a narrative of lives and agricultural processes. The cultural context and references of these resources are those of contemporary popular culture – movies, games, comic strips, and the linguistic register of children's television.

The two screens look very different, and construct themselves as screen differently. The Cadbury's screen looks backward to the book – to the educational magazine, the Maths textbook, the printed, text-heavy worksheet. The Dubble site looks forward – to the multiple connections of hypertext, to the participatory pleasures of the computer game, to the visual drama of the moving image, and to a curriculum which doesn't stop at the school gates, in which children slip easily in and out of school mode, finding resources in both to explore and construct their world.

However, in spite of their differences, the sites retain similarities. As remarked upon at the beginning of this chapter, both are selling an ethical message and a commercial product. While both offer information, then, ostensibly in a spirit of educational neutrality, both employ the visual rhetorics in particular of advertising – the logos, the constant and varied representation of the product in traditional child-friendly iconographies, and a specific naming function of language, through, in particular, the words 'Dubble' and 'Cadbury'. This is an economic and educational battle fought out with similar advertising tools, but with very different articulations of the available digital resources.

Methodological points

1. The analysis of still-image design, as demonstrated by Kress and Van Leuween (1996), is also a useful initial approach to webpage design. It is important to add to this approach the

additional aspects of embedded links within pages and the pathways they offer the user. In relation to this question, Lemke (2002) suggests how the concept of multimodality can be developed into one of *hypermodality*.

2. Testing out the variety of choices users make when interacting with the same webpage could form the basis of a small-scale research project. Filming traversals over the shoulder of users is possible, but does not capture screen detail (e.g. cursor movement) well. Screen capture software, which can also record the voice of the user, can be more useful.

3. The spoken comments of the user can then be analysed as part of the whole multimodal event (see Chapter 5 on analysing interview data). Screen-capture software can produce the events on the screen as a multimedia-format movie, with the voice of the users at the keyboard as its soundtrack. The articulation of voice with cursor movement, click-decisions and link activation can then all be analysed clearly.

Acknowledgement

This chapter forms part of the research project *LEARNING ONLINE: e-learning and the domestic market*, funded by the Economic and Social Research Council, 2002–3.

4

Returning to Hogwarts: The Modality of Computer Games

The box of the computer game of *Harry Potter and the Chamber of Secrets* (Electronic Arts, 2002) addresses us in a way no text other than a computer game can. It says: 'DARE YOU RETURN TO HOGWARTS? BE HARRY POTTER™ AND UNLOCK THE MYSTERY AT THE HEART OF THE CHAMBER OF SECRETS.' We can look at this exhortation in terms of the system known as *modality*: how texts make truth-claims – claims for credibility. As Kress and van Leeuwen (1996) point out, these claims are not part of the *representational* function of the text; they are not representing an objective truth in the world. Rather, they are part of the *orientational* function – they are the text's attempt to address its audience as part of a community which shares a set of beliefs about how the world is.

In the statement above, then, the modality stakes its claim to truth on a kind of believable fiction – that the listener will assent to the demand, and agree to pretend to be Harry Potter. This is a dramatic modality, central to role-playing and action adventure games where the player controls a character in the game. Ordinary narrative lays out a series of events as statements: the indicative mood in language, which the French narratologist Gerard Genette says is the natural mood of narrative (Genette, 1980). This invitation to join the game is expressed as a command: 'BE Harry Potter'. The imperative mood may be the natural mood of games.

The exhortation contains two names: Harry Potter and Hogwarts. No sense can be made of these without an intertextual understanding, which allows us to recognize them as, respectively, a boy wizard and his school of witchcraft and wizardy. This can only be credible in a community which recognizes the modality of fantasy – an impossible world which we agree, in certain ways, to treat as real. We also know that fantasy is a form of fiction with a particular historical role in children's literature and film, and that it may be believable to children for different reasons and in different ways than will be the case with adults.

Finally, this game will also contain a modality value related to how authentic it seems as a game. The modality of games as cultural events is always an issue. The spectacle of wrestling, for instance, projects a contested modality, so that fans or practitioners of 'real' amateur wrestling will perceive the professional wrestling of the WWF as a dramatic fiction.

In the case of *Harry Potter and the Chamber of Secrets* this kind of authenticity may be judged against two quite separate generic characters of the game: its credibility as a role-playing or adventure game; and its credibility as a transformation of a Harry Potter narrative. Experienced gamers may judge the game on its authenticity as a game; while Harry Potter fans, conversely, might judge the game on how faithful it is to the other parts of the franchise. This reviewer recognizes the tension:

> The game does follow the book and may trigger some wonderful memories of J. K. Rowling's amazing work. The good news is that the game follows the story. Like the *Fellowship of the Ring* . . . this is also somewhat limiting to the overall gameplay.
>
> (www.gamezone.com)

Following van Leeuwen, we will regard this kind of modality as *presentational*, that is the claim of the text to be true to its genre, as distinct from its represented world:

In the case of representation, 'truth' means 'a true representation of the people, places and/or things represented', in the case of presentation it means 'true to the spirit of the genre, and the values which underpin it in its context'.

(van Leeuwen, 1999)

Because computer games are hybrid forms, they construct hybrid modalities. A good deal of debate in the field of games studies revolves around a perceived opposition between narratology (the study of narrative) and ludology (the study of games). This chapter will take the simple way out of this dilemma by assuming that role-playing and action adventure games necessarily combine the two. However, as well as providing the mainspring for the game's interactive pleasures, this also causes complex modality tensions.

We will analyse the game, then, from two perspectives – the *narrative* and the *ludic* (as well as considering its presentational modality). In assessing how these two systems build the hybrid modality of the game, we will refer to Kress and van Leeuwen's notion of how modal orientations are proposed by a text and judged by an audience (Kress and van Leeuwen, 1996). They suggest four modality coding orientations:

- *naturalistic* – in which the text's truth claim and the audience's judgment of it are based on representational similarity to the natural world or aspects of it
- *sensory* – in which modality is based on how effective the text is in eliciting an emotional response through appeal to different sensory channels
- *abstract* – the modality of high art and science, for instance, which aims to represent essences of things through sparse, stripped down signs (the opposite, in a way, of the naturalistic modality)
- *technological* – the modality based on utility, as in a technical manual or a map

47

Though Kress and van Leeuwen's schema are applied to visual modes, van Leeuwen uses the same framework to analyse the modalities of music and sound (van Leeuwen, 1999). We will see how it can be adapted for the multiplicity of modes integrated in the computer game.

Before beginning the analysis, we should indicate why analysing computer games might be relevant to educational research. There are, broadly, two perspectives in the literature relating games to education. One is largely social, looking at how games feature in the cultural lives of young people; and sometimes highlighting gendered uses of games in which girls are disadvantaged (Orr-Vered, 1998; Mackereth and Anderson, 2000). The other perspective is to view games as a form of communicative competence or literacy, linked to the development of print literacy (Beavis, 2001; McClay, 2002). The framework we propose in this chapter allows for the analysis of games as semiotic systems, either to consider what they offer children; or to consider how children engage with them (perhaps in conjunction with an empirical study of players); or to consider how they might be understood as a textual form worthy of inclusion in the curriculum.

Narrative modality

The game presents its narrative through two forms of the kineikonic, or moving image, mode – interactive and non-interactive. In semiotic terms, non-interactive elements of the text will require the player to read and interpret the information on the screen, but not necessarily to produce any external semiotic transformations. If external signs (spoken comment, laughter or writing) are produced, they will not be returned into the semiotic system of the text. Interactive elements, by contrast, can only work by the production of external signs by the player which *are* returned into the game system, which then responds, the player responding again to this response, and so on (the feedback loop or information loop of Human-Computer Interaction theory).

The non-interactive kineikonic

This is the mode of the 'cut-scenes' – short films which fulfil various functions, most importantly, filling in narrative information, and giving instructions about how to play the game. However, the narrative information, visual style and temporal flow all interrelate with the interactive sequences, so the two must be considered together.

As in the interactive elements of the game, the cut scenes project a general modality which corresponds to the naturalistic coding orientation of Kress and van Leeuwen (1996). This orientation, they suggest, will be set up in the text (and judged by the viewer) using *modality configurations* which express degrees on a scale which allows for higher or lower modality in each parameter. Of the eight configurations they propose, we will select three:

- articulation of detail
- articulation of background
- colour saturation

We will apply these to an image from a cut scene in which the Professor of Defence Against the Dark Arts, Gilderoy Lockhart, is teaching Harry and the rest of the class to duel using magic spells. In respect of the three modality configurations, we can make the following observations:

- Detail is clearly articulated in the character design; Lockhart has blond, wavy hair, his eyes blink naturalistically; the buttons on his yellow coat are clearly defined. However, we recognize this as as animation which, while in some respects it aspires to the naturalistic modality of photographic realism, has a distinctive visual aesthetic which has become part

49

of the stylistic conventions of computer games, perceived by players as 'graphics' rather than, say, as video.

- The articulation of the background presents a high natural-istic modality (we can even see the fine-grained texture of the stone walls in the Defence Against the Dark Arts classroom).
- The colours are bright, highly-saturated.

Kress and van Leeuwen suggest that colour saturation and articulation of detail greater than the photographic standard of the time presents a modality which moves beyond the 'real', provoking a sense of 'more-than-real' which they associate with fantasy genres. Here, this kind of hyper-real modality (with the less-than-real animation) is part of the construction of fantasy, a world that is imaginary, but also brighter and more solid than the physical world we inhabit – or at least than images judged to be accurate representations of that world.

The game, like the book and film, shows children who both are and are not like real children. Many children's fantasies over the last hundred years construct a mixed modality of fantasy and realism, by combining signifiers of social reality such as contemporary dress and speech codes with signifiers of fantasy. E. Nesbit's novels are a good example, mixing the speech patterns and realist settings of Edwardian childhood with fantasy images of phoenixes and flying carpets. C. S. Lewis's novels adopt a similar strategy; and J. K. Rowling follows this tradition. Harry's broomstick, the Nimbus 2000, is a semiotic yoking together of signifiers which suggests an object belonging both to a world of fantasy and magic, and to a world of contemporary logo-branded sports gear.

The cut scenes continue this mixed modality, as we have seen. The visual design makes fantasy believable through an exaggerated naturalism. The player is positioned as a child character with a particular relation to the adult world; that of a pupil, in the scene discussed above. Elsewhere we are addressed by the voice of the narrator, the English comic actor Stephen

Fry, whose use of a slightly old-fashioned received pronunci-
ation and mellifluous tones convey a reassuring adult presence.
The players are invited to take their places as child-listeners
waiting for a narrative whose style and tone of address con-
firms a particular kind of representation of English childhood,
in which log fires blaze, manorial buildings offer refuge from
the stultifying dullness of suburban life, and orphaned children
find a new family in the fantasy world of wizards, and the peer-
companionship of the boarding school. By contrast, the
vaguely London accents of the non-player child-characters
(except Hermione) suggest the more diverse school population
of the contemporary state comprehensive school.

We will also make some brief observations about the modalities of sound, movement and spatio-temporal structures in this
sequence:

- The sound combines a high naturalistic modality (speech
  pitch and dynamics synced with the image suggesting a 'real'
  person; footsteps and other naturalistic sounds) with music
  derived from the film, built around an abstract-sensory
  modality suggesting magic and the supernatural (through a
  haunting minor melody, with eerie string instrumentation),
  as well as childhood (through the associations of 3 : 4 time, and
  this particular melody, with nursery rhyme and lullaby).
- The movements are, like all those in the cut scenes, in principle unrestricted. Because these scenes are not part of the
  gameplay, or interactive in any way, they can represent
  movement unrestrictedly, like any animation. Here, Lockhart's movements are largely gestural, and complement the
  naturalistic modality of the visual design and the dialogue.
- Temporally and spatially, the cut scenes are constructed
  according to the conventions of continuity editing (see
  Bordwell and Thompson, 2001). Time and space are frag-
  mented in shots, which are then edited together to construct
  an effect of continuous present time, as in this sequence.
  Though this chopping-up of time is by no means an

51

analogue of real-world time and space, continuity editing presents it as such, and we learn to read it as such; to assent, in effect, to a naturalistic modality.

In summary, we can see that the different modes of the kineikonic complement each other to build a high naturalistic modality, which at times exceeds the natural, suggesting the more-than-real world of fantasy. We will also judge this by what we know of real schools and fictional schools – a combined modality of what we recognize as like our school experience and like the rather different school experience of Harry Potter (and the boarding school genre of children's fiction), in which we agree to believe – or not.

Alongside this representational modality is the different modality of the game's claim to authenticity as a game, its *presentational* modality.

The detailed articulation of the visual design produces a credible-looking computer game. In this player review, the basis for the modality judgement of the visual design (under the heading 'Graphics') is a judgment about how the game presents itself as a game, so that it becomes the kind of judgment of authenticity, or presentational modality, we described earlier:

> Graphics: TERRIFIC! The art direction on this project is EXCELLENT! This is a visually stunning game!
>
> (www.videogamereview.com)

Presentationally, cut scenes may be judged in drastically differing ways: by players who enjoy the cinematic quality of games, for whom a high modality would rest on the feeling that the game allows them to become part of a movie; or by players for whom the formal systems of the game produce the highest modality, so that the cut scenes become a pointless distraction from the game. Game designers recognize these two orientations – many games, including this one, lavish considerable design effort on the cut scenes as well as including in the game a simple mechanism for the player to skip them, in this case by pressing the 'enter' key.

From cut scene to gameplay – the player-avatar link

However, cut scenes and game play cannot simply be analysed as independent elements – they are clearly interrelated, and able to affect each other's semiotic structures, including modality systems, so that, ideally, the gameplay takes on a little more of the cinematic quality while the cut scene acquires some of the features of the game.

Like many games, this one trains its players at the outset of the game. Trainee players are often positioned in game culture and by the text as 'newbies', through linguistic or visual representations of the ideas of training, initiation and newness. In *The Chamber of Secrets*, these representations are associated with the game's representations of school. The player is trained in the use of spells by teachers in the narrative, attending lessons in spellcraft of various kinds, and so are invited to become game-trainee and Hogwarts pupil simultaneously.

In this cut scene, then, the game, through the figure of Gilderoy Lockhart, says: 'There are three spells you may use in duelling . . .' and continues to instruct Harry how to duel against Draco Malfoy.

There are two kinds of second-person address here – the use of the word 'you' in Lockhart's dialogue; and the way the image looks out of the screen at us – what Kress and van Leeuwen call 'a kind of visual you'. The conventions of continuity editing tell us that Lockhart is addressing Harry, since the images of Lockhart talking are intercut with 'reaction shots' of Harry, Ron and Hermione listening. However, as Lockhart's instructions proceed, something odd happens, disrupting the modality and orientation of the text. Lockhart tells us that the power of the spell cast by the wand can be increased by holding down the left mouse button. It is as if the mechanisms of address in the text suddenly turn outwards, as we realize that, though the character of Harry is being addressed by Lockhart, we, who hold the mouse, are also being addressed.

At this point, the representational and orientational structures of the text operate to pull Harry and the player together. We are about to become Harry through the dramatic guise of the avatar. ('Avatar', the word for the player-controlled character in a game, is derived from a Sanskrit word denoting the descent of a god to earth in human form.)

We can say three things about modality here.

Firstly, games do not operate the same kind of naturalistic modality as films, or mentioning the computer hardware would be completely unacceptable, much as if a cowboy in a Western were to look out of the screen and tell the projectionist to change the reel. As we shall see, games involve a combination of naturalistic, sensory and technological modalities, and players learn to combine these – so the instruction about the mouse is simply a part of the technological modality running alongside the naturalistic modality of the kineikonic mode.

Secondly, however, the explicit mention of the mouse is strictly a part of this technological orientation as it is constructed in the early part of the game. The modality of the game expects players, in this training phase, to learn explicitly about the technological utility of the controls, very like someone learning to drive. And just as drivers later manage the controls in ways we describe as 'intuitive', 'unconscious', 'without thinking', or 'automatic', so the developing modality of the game encourages us to forget the controls, so that by the time we are fighting the big battles against Aragog the giant spider, or the basilisk in the Chamber of Secrets, we are barely aware of the mouse. The technological modality is judged by how unobtrusive it is, so that it blends with the naturalistic – the computer mediation is meant to become invisible, and we feel we are really firing off spells or wielding the sword of Gryffindor.

Thirdly, the language of Lockhart's dialogue contains specific modality cues. The use of the word 'you' raises the ludic modality as we are included as participants in the systems of game and narrative. The word 'may' is a modal auxiliary, part of the system of modality in language which expresses degrees of certainty. In this case, though it seems to produce a weak modality within what is basically a set of instructions, it may be there to soften what is actually an imperative: 'Use these three spells.' Dressing up a command as an invitation is typical of the language of teachers, who need to be sensitive about how instructions are felt by pupils, and in this respect it is an appropriate representation of a teacher at Hogwarts talking to Harry Potter. However, games are also, in many ways, sets of instructions – rule-governed systems which tell us what to do. But modality systems determine how we want to perceive these rules, an obvious example being the imposition of a penalty by a football referee, perceived as fair (high modality) by one team's supporters, and unfair (low modality) by the other's. Similarly, the instructions offered by the ludic pedagogy of *The Chamber of Secrets* will seem like an exciting invitation to those who subscribe to its world, culture and community; and constraining, clumsy, imperious or patronizing to those who do not.

As the cut scene finishes, we move into a gameplay sequence, in this case the duel of Harry against Draco. In the next section, we will consider how the modality of gameplay integrates the kineikonic modality systems we have already looked at with other systems, so that narrative and game are fused.

Ludic modality

The gameplay sequences operate hybrid modalities, which can to some extent be analysed using three of Kress and van Leeuwen's categories: naturalistic, sensory and technological.

Naturalistic

A part of this modality is created using the same resources as in the cut scenes – visual detail, background articulation, high colour saturation, use of naturalistic sounds and, in all of this, a tendency to move the naturalism higher up the scale towards the more-than-real register of fantasy.

However, there are important structural differences which make the sense of reality, or the credibility of this fantasy world, differently constructed. Most importantly, we are now working the controls of the avatar, and imagine ourselves as Harry Potter, if the modality is high enough in our judgement.

Firstly, we observe that the image typical of the cut scene – a face looking out of the screen at us (to offer, instruct and inform) – has been reversed. The typical image of the game-sequences contains, in the foreground, the figure of Harry seen from behind, so that we look over his shoulder at the scene confronting us. As in most action adventure games (one of the best-known being the *Tomb Raider* series), the player is located in a fixed position with respect to the avatar, placed immediately behind him. This means we are always facing the same way as Harry, once removed from looking through his eyes. This position constructs a complex sense that the player is both identified with Harry Potter and once removed from him, able to watch him, but linked with him like a shadow.

Secondly, we can now perform a limited repertoire of actions: RUN (forwards, backwards, left and right), JUMP and CAST SPELLS. This is a *restricted set*; unlike the actions depicted in the cut scenes, where, precisely because actions do not depend on the limitations of player controls, Harry can do anything. The point of gameplay is that the character can perform very few actions, which are wielded with skill by players. The linguist M. A. K. Halliday described the 'restricted language' of games, his example being contract bridge, where limited formulae in the bidding system offer a meaning potential. Saying 'three clubs' in the right circumstances would, in spite of the restricted nature of the resources, represent considerable skill (Halliday, 1974). The player develops the skills to employ the 'language' of Harry's action repertoire to engage in typical game-like activities – exploring, puzzle-solving, quest-like activities, combat and collecting.

Though the modality invoked here is a technological one – the gameplay is credible if it gets us through the obstacle course – it also links with the naturalistic modality of the world represented by the moving image. It might seem that the limited, formulaic set of actions would lower the naturalistic modality, making the avatar look artificial, mechanical and inhuman. In fact, for players who base their modality judgments on evaluations of this repertoire compared with other games offering more variety, such a judgment is possible, as in this review:

> Gameplay: The gameplay is BORRRRRRING. It's a lot like watching paint dry. Walk around . . . LOAD . . . walk around some more . . . LOAD . . . collects some frog, beans or balloons . . . LOAD . . . Solve a puzzle . . . walk around again . . . get the picture?
>
> (www.videogamereview.com)

When we consider that this player is the same one who enthused over the visual design of the game, we can see that the hybrid modalities of game and narrative can produce violently mixed modality judgments in players.

However, the restricted repertoire of movements is not necessarily experienced as limiting. Though the meaning potential looks sparse, every move is different because it causes a different conjunction of the moving character and a part of the gameworld. So, the same move forward in different contexts can bring us to a yawning precipice, through the lab of Professor Snape, between the tentacles of the Venomous Tentacula plant, up to a schoolmate who offers to trade with us, or into contact with a bubbling cauldron where Harry will mix a health-restoring potion. These moves are two-term syntagms (sequences of signs), consisting of a single movement forwards (the 'up' arrow key on the PC keyboard), combined with an object in the gameworld. Each combination implies a different action in the player perception where in mechanical terms there is only one, so the semiotic value of the single movement is expanded from 'move forward' to 'teeter', 'tiptoe', 'dash', 'approach' and 'mix' in the situations described above.

Two signifying systems associated with the kineikonic are in play here. Firstly, the succession of syntagms combining represented actor and location or background through animated movement; and secondly, the camera positions which locate the viewer. Unlike the conventional kineikonic structures, which are fixed at the point of viewing, these structures are dynamic, and controlled by the player. So the sense of 'teetering' created by the combination of a move forward and a precipice is enhanced if the player rotates the camera vertically (using the mouse in the PC version) so as to look down on Harry's head, and directly into the precipice. In many ways, this naturalism is completely the opposite to the conventions of continuity editing. Space and time are no longer constructed by disjuncture and editing, but by continuous exploration of 3-D space. This is 'real-time' – there can be no contraction, expansion or omission. In cinematic terms, it is like a continuous single take.

While the modality dominant in all of these examples continues to be the heightened naturalism of fantasy, this needs to be complemented by a notion of dramatic modality: the modality contract between game and player is more like drama than it is like a picture, a book or a film. We agree, as we said at the beginning of this chapter, to pretend to be Harry Potter, to play a role. Brenda Laurel (1993) and Janet Murray (1997) both imagine computer gameplay as being like a theatre audience who are allowed to step over the edge of the stage and play a part. Many of the modality configurations we have described should contribute to a high dramatic modality. On the other hand, there are elements of the game's systems which may serve to detract from the dramatic sense of 'being' Harry. One obvious such element is that the game engine constructs Harry as a single-player character, where in other games the player can control a team of characters. This results in Harry's missions being rather isolated affairs – he only communicates with Hermione and Ron in the cut scenes, that is, not at all as far as the player's participation is concerned. Some of the affective satisfaction of a group of children pitting their wits agains the adult world in a spirit of comradeship is necessarily undermined by the solo avatar structure, which might lower the dramatic modality for players to whom the representations of friendship in the book and film are important.

Sensory modality

Literally, of course, we are only inputting mechanical instructions which are processed by the game engine. The modality here, then, depends on our interpretation of these events through the semiotic guise of the game – the images and sounds clothing the skeleton of the game-system. The higher the modality, the more we believe we are 'really' running, climbing, falling, mixing, fighting and flying. Here is an example of a player for whom the combination of the naturalistic modality of the semiotic guise and the technological modality of the interactive controls produces a high sensory modality:

> Graphics were better than i imagined. When you fly your broom around hogwarts the detail is very crisp and clear. Down to the water splashing in your face when flying close to the lake.
>
> (www.videogamereview.com)

There is no sense here that the player is at all aware of the fact that the 'flying' is 'really' the pressing of four directional keys on a control. When the feeling of being completely involved in the game is as strong as in this example, the modality shifts. This is not just a feeling that the gameworld seems real; it is a

59

sensory, emotional response. This very high sensory modality seems to depend, in turn, on a naturalistic orientation and a technological orientation, in Kress and van Leeuwen's terms (1996). It may even be that the interactive element requires a new conception of modality based in the experience of 'flow' – perhaps a *sensory-kinaesthetic* orientation, where the emotional rush of acting in the represented world depends on the play-ability of the controls as well as the visual detail, 3-D rendering, enhanced sound and the other articulations that serve as cues for the naturalistic and sensory modalities.

Technological modality

The sensory experience of this player depends on the credible blend of naturalistic image and sound (the kineikonic mode) with a technological modality which depends on the invisibility of the controls. However, to believe wholeheartedly in the game is not only to become immersed in a naturalistic modality. Other elements of the game are represented by much less naturalistic visual design. At any time in the game, the player can move from the gameworld to the inventory screen, which is a typical generic element of role-playing games.

The inventory (like the map screen, also typical of the role-playing game genre) operates Kress and van Leeuwen's technological coding orientation. Here, a lack of detail, icon-like representation of objects or processes and flat-colour construct the modality, judged by how clearly and usefully we can see and deploy the resources available to us in the game. So, for instance, at the top left hand side, the combination of image (a flask) and number (1) tell us we have one potion left with which to restore life to our character. When we move back into the game, we may need to drink this potion in order to survive a battle. The link is indicated by the lightning flash graphic at the top of the game screen, which tells us how much health we have left. If the narrative modality is high, we are likely to believe in this feeling of health; and the sense of urgency this injects into the performance of actions, especially in the combat sequences, shifts us from a technological modality back into the play between the naturalistic modality of the game-narrative (believing we are Harry Potter) and the sensory modality of performing his actions, itself enhanced by our adrenalin rush as the health meter runs down.

The technological modality is clearly signalled by our active representative on the screen, which is no longer the avatar, but the cursor (though in the form of a wand, to represent the avatar symbolically). As in Lockhart's mention of the mouse, the technological modality happily acknowledges the computer-mediated nature of the gameplay.

This modality is likely to be judged on a number of scales in computer games. One scale is what we will call dynamic density – what number and variety of functions can be performed. Another might be ludic or narrative versatility – how many different actions a single function can achieve. On these kinds of measure, the central technologies of the game – the avatar movements, the wand targeting, and the health restoration – might be predicted to produce a high ludic and narrative modality, as we have seen in the case of the player for whom these modalities in turn produced a sensory experience. They are economic functions which, in combination with the gameworld, produce a wide and satisfying diversity of events.

The inventory, by contrast, might produce a low ludic modality. It contains a very restricted dynamic density – the map contains little detail and the objects represented on the inventory screen are there to inform rather than to be manipulated. A major function is to allow players to check on how many 'wizard cards' they have collected, which suggests that the modality of the inventory is designed to appeal to the collecting instinct in children, much as the Pokemon phenomenon did. This aspect of the technological modality appeals to the presentational authenticity of the game as a part of its

61

audience's culture, rather than on the basis of its truth to the book or film.

Conclusion: the modality of children's games

The overall modality of the game, then, depends on the articulation of these three modal orientations. The *technological* allows us to feel we can control the game and manage its economies; the *naturalistic* allows us to blend the narrative and the player-controlled actions and projects the fantasy world of Hogwarts; and the *sensory* reaches its peak at the moments when the blend of narrative action and game-system works best. It seems that the high naturalistic modality of the 3-D visual environment, allied with the high technological and sensory modalities of the player-controlled events, can produce a vivid, dramatic experience of being Harry Potter, in the fantasy world of Hogwarts. However, we have also seen that such modality structures offer meaning potentials to players, who might judge either the overall modality of the game or its constituent modalities quite differently. While in some cases the blend of naturalistic and technological modalities may create a convincing sense of dramatic engagement with the avatar and his world, in other ways it may not, as in the isolation of Harry from Hermione and Ron by the solo avatar structure.

We have also seen that the authenticity claim, or presentational modality, is a wider one, intertextual both in its reference to the Harry Potter franchise more generally, and in its reference to other games. As a game, the combination of naturalistic, sensory and technological modalities seem to be satisfying, but to offer in some cases experiences which are clearly directed at the game-culture of younger children, such as the collecting mechanisms, and the simplicity of the single-player character. Here, clearly, modality judgments will depend on the community the player belongs to.

As a component in the wider Harry Potter text family, the

game's modality appeal both draws on and is measured by the profound credibility of the books for large numbers of children, producing the kind of fan communities more typical of popular television and film series (Borah, 2003). This brand loyalty, expressive of a kind of generic baseline modality, remains steady even where the game is specifically found wanting – indeed, it seems to be a modality standard against which the game is judged:

> Then I got into Hogwarts and realised this was not the game for me. First off, at night at least, the place is roaming with ghosts. I figured the ghosts were there for atmosphere. In the book the spirits are by and large friendly and unobtrusive (the poltergeist excepted of course :)). Here, they will harm you if you contact one!
>
> (www.videogamereview.com)

For this player, the naturalistic and sensory modalities are high – even too high – while the presentational modality of the game and its truth to the book is low.

In the end, we cannot say in what specific ways children will respond to the mix of fantasy and realist modalities in the game without extending our research to an empirical study of child players. However, we can, at least, say that the mix is there on offer in the text, extended into a participatory, dramatic experience by the sensory and technological modalities of the game.

Methodological points

1. It is difficult to subject a computer game to textual analysis in the same way as a film or book, since the text only exists as gameplay sessions, which are always different. Options open to the researcher are to relate the analysis to screen grabs; or to record gameplay sessions, either with a camera over the player's shoulder or using screen-capture software, which can produce the gameplay session as a multimedia format

movie. This will, of course, not simply produce the game as a text to be analysed, but will produce a particular traversal by a player, offering another dimension for analysis.

2. To extend the research investigation into the player's experience, many possibilities are open. The researcher can observe and film the players during play (see Schott and Horrell, 2000). The players can be interviewed, and the interviews analysed within the multimodal framework (see Chapter 5).

3. Or the researcher can collect examples of players' online cultures, from review websites, tribute websites, online communities and so on. If online games are being analysed, the researcher will, of course, meet other players within the game, in the form of avatars, which raises the intriguing possibility of interviewing players online in role! These interviews can, of course, be recorded using screen-capture software, as described above. There are questions to think about in online research relating to the researcher's role and presence – do you announce your identity as a researcher; do you regard your presence as a digital equivalent of the participant observer role in ethnographic research; or do you behave as a *bona fide* member of the online community and conceal your research identity? These are questions of researcher role and ethics which are only just beginning to be addressed in the context of the internet.

5

Transforming Hannibal: Interview Data and Textual Analysis

We have seen in the three previous chapters how multimodal approaches can make possible an analysis of texts which is attentive to their deployment of different semiotic modes and to their functions as texts. So far, however, we have paid less attention to what happens to these texts when they are picked up by those who want to use them or engage with them – audiences, spectators, readers and players. The range of words possible to describe those who engage with texts reflects both an emphasis on specific modes (hearing, watching, reading and playing), and can also suggest particular economic positionings (as in a *target audience*). In the tradition of Cultural Studies there is a long history of empirical research which observes how real audiences use texts of various kinds. The general upshot of this tradition is to demonstrate that audiences are not as passive, as easily fooled, or as inexorably positioned by texts, ideologies or state forces as was once thought. In particular, the work of David Buckingham has shown how important it is to pay attention to child audiences, whose voices are easily lost beneath the weight of adults who speak and interpret on their behalf (Buckingham, 2000). Multimodal theory, which is broadly aligned with the emphasis in Cultural Studies on the agency of audiences and on the legitimacy of the pleasures they derive from texts, sees audiences as active makers of meaning, though in a more literal sense. It sees 'reading' as a form of 'design'.

How can multimodal analysis be employed in the study of audiences?

In educational research a common question is: 'How do children engage with texts?' The methods most frequently used to explore this question are forms of discourse analysis, using what children say in interviews, in naturally occurring conversation or what they write about texts, and forms of sociological research which interpret interview data, field observations, visual and other material evidence and so on, to build a picture of social and cultural behaviours and engagement with texts within these contexts.

Multimodality offers a different perspective. Instead of regarding children's talk or writing as a self-contained mode of communication to be analysed using separate methodologies from those used to analyse texts, it asks two questions. Firstly, how is this talk or writing combined with other semiotic modes and media to convey its message? Secondly, how are these forms of communication semiotically related to the text with which they engage?

In other words, the text and the reader's engagement with it, expressed through language (but also whatever other modes are available and useful), can be analysed using the same multimodal theory. Text and the reader's semiotic work on the text can be seen as a continuum rather than as two separate kinds of signification.

An important background to this discussion is Kress and van Leeuwen's argument (2001) that the interpretation of texts is itself a form of sign production, even a form of design. In this view, the text makes available a set of semiotic resources in different modes and media, which the reader, spectator or player must make sense of through semiotic work in their own head. When you watch a film, in your head you can remake it principally in the form of visual images; when you read a story, you may work on it in your head through a combination of words and images, though in this case the images are provided by you. Already certain kinds of transformation are happening.

Very often this kind of internal sign production will become externalized, and it is at this point that it becomes accessible to the researcher. When audiences externalize their interpretation, they reach for the resources at hand. So when people come out of a cinema, they will use language and gesture to exchange their ideas and feelings about the film they have just seen. In a classroom, children may be asked to write about a book or a film, though increasingly they may be asked to design a poster or make a video trailer as well. Other resources have become available.

The text, then, offers itself as a narrative, argument or other propositional sequence, using particular multimodal and multimedial combinations. The reader interprets and responds through a process of internal sign production. In many cases, these interpretations are then externalized and transformed again.

We will use the example of a seventeen-year-old sixth-form student talking about his viewing of a film.

Chris and Hannibal

In this example, a boy is talking about his viewing of the film *Hannibal* (Scott, 2000). In Kress and van Leeuwen's terms, the internal 'take' on the text he might have had when he saw the film has become transformed over time, and is now being reconstructed as an external utterance. In the interview, conducted by the present authors in 2001, Chris tells us that he saw the film with a group of friends about six months previously. In general, his account seems typical of popular cinema audiences – he is much more aware of the star of the film than the director, and is not aware that this film has a different director than *Silence of the Lambs* (Demme, 1991). He is also not aware at all of the earlier manifestation of Lecter played by Brian Cox in *Manhunter* (Mann, 1986), which is cited approvingly by another student in the same interview (who is also keenly aware of Ridley Scott as the director of *Hannibal*). These are the kinds of cultural orientation to cinema demonstrated by the French sociologist Pierre Bourdieu in his encyclopaedic mapping of cultural taste in France (Bourdieu, 1987). In Bourdieu's account, being aware of a film by star rather than director would suggest a popular aesthetic orientation rather than the elite aesthetic of art-house cinema, or the interpretive strategies of an academic audience.

Another feature of Chris's account is his admiring attitude to Hannibal. This can be seen in the context of how the audiences of popular horror films position themselves in relation to the monsters of the genre. Carol Clover, arguing from a psychoanalytical perspective, argues that horror audiences are essentially masochistic, and identify with the victims of the monster (Clover, 1993). Clover's work, however, rests on an ideal conception of the audience rather than on evidence from real audiences. David Buckingham, whose work, by contrast, researches actual teenage audiences, finds evidence which partly supports Clover's thesis of victim-identified audiences, but also evidence of more mobile forms of identification, where viewers' sympathies shift in complex ways between the monster and the victims (Buckingham, 1996).

We will analyse in some detail one extract from the interview with Chris. As well as looking at how the representational function of his talk transforms representational aspects of the film, we will look at how the orientational function of his interview both engages with orientational aspects of the film, and is directed towards two different kinds of interpretive community – the friends with whom he saw the film; and the researchers now talking to him.

Here is the extract from the video transcript:

AB: How about you, Chris, what did you –
Chris: Well, um, the detective went into Hannibal's apartment, and that's – don't really know why that's my

favourite, it's probably cos – it shows like how normal he can be – and – in the back of your mind you're worried about the detective, whether he's gonna kill him, he could've so easily killed him and had him for breakfast – and – he just goes into his apartment and helps him with his suitcase, um, cos when they, cos Starling's come in from America, to come and get him, and this detective's helping him to leave, and you see, you hear the classical music and he's, um, like, sitting there, like explaining everything, and it shows his normal side, and he's er, cos he's very rich, he's a very rich person, so it shows his, um upper-class side, and then you go and see when he kills the detective, I dunno what his name is, um, it shows his, um violent side as well – like he's just finished a lecture on history, and, er, man who had his guts cut out [*draws finger across stomach*], and was hung from a tree, just finished a lecture, and then he goes and kills someone, like the two – mercenaries, I think he slits one of their throats [*draws finger across throat*], and then er he puts, um, the detective on a truck and throws him – er, little wheelchair thing [*complex two handed movement representing putting on and throwing off*] and throws him off the edge – kind of shows a contrast, that really – that's the bit I most enjoyed, where you see the difference of character.

Representation

There are three main representational threads in Chris's talk.

Firstly, there are clauses which are built round the actions of Lecter and his victim in the film: 'the detective went into Hannibal's apartment'; 'he slits one of their throats'; 'he puts, um, the detective on a truck'. We could interpret this strand as being dominated by the logic of narrative. Its representational purpose is to – literally – re-present the story, turning the moving images of Lecter and Pazzi on the screen into noun-phrases which function as the actors in his clauses, related to verb phrases which transform the actions in the film into their verbal equivalents.

To re-present the narrative, several highly selective mechanisms are at work. Firstly, to select this sequence as his favourite part of the film; secondly, to select the salient parts for his purpose and to transpose them into the mode of spoken language; and thirdly, to select relevant sections from other moments of the narrative, establishing forms of narrative causality which lead into this episode ('cos Starling's come in from America, to come and get him . . .') and out of it ('just finished a lecture, and then he goes and kills someone . . .').

The use of the gestural mode plays an important part, too. The disembowelling and chair-tipping gestures Chris makes amplify these important moments of the narrative; but they also compensate for the difficulty language has in representing the complexity of physical action. The mode employed by the film for this kind of representation is that of dramatic action; Chris reaches for the closest mode available to him, mime, in re-presenting these powerful moments. He selects and combines moments of intense physical horror, the mime reworking the visual semiotic of the moving image, stitching together and condensing actions which will emphasize the genre and the monster who grips Chris's imagination.

Secondly, however, there is another ideational structure at work which is by no means simply about the re-presentation of narrative, but about the proposal of more abstract structures. This is the idea of a kind of dual identity in Lecter's character – its monstrous aspect, contrasted with what Chris terms his 'normal' side.

This second representational strand of Chris's account sets up a structure of contrasts, specifically in four clauses. These all begin with 'it shows': 'it shows how normal he can be'; 'it shows his normal side'; 'it shows his, um, upper-class side'; and 'kind of shows a contrast, that really – that's the bit I most enjoyed, where you see the difference of character'. The theme of these clauses is not narration, but the act of interpretation. The verb 'shows' emphasizes this act, linking it with the citation of evidence.

These clauses are not independent or random – they are structurally related, in a two-part contrast Chris is setting up between the 'normal' Lecter and the violent murderer. This contrast is made explicit towards the end. However, it is a clear ideational structure incorporating the more narrative clauses, which, it appears now, are not simply a re-telling of the story, but are cited as evidence for this contrastive structure.

The third kind of representation is a representation of the act of viewing. These sequences begin with 'You' or 'I' – the spectator, either a generalized spectator or Chris himself, is represented as the actor, in the act of spectating. These representations make a quite specific distinction between two different kinds of interpretation. Those attributed to 'I' are forms of interpretation which are personal, which cannot be reliably attributed to spectators in general. This is, here, either because of doubt – 'I dunno what his name is' – or because of an affective engagement which cannot be assumed for other viewers – 'That's the bit I really enjoyed.'

Orientation

We need to read Chris's interpretation as having a double orientation. Firstly, it must express an orientation to the text, which meets the orientational structures offered by the text. The film sequence here locates us closer to Pazzi – the camera tracks him as he enters the apartment, keeping Lecter hidden to begin with, so that the audience becomes anxious about his whereabouts just as Pazzi does. We are shocked with Pazzi at the abrupt appearance of Lecter, signalled by the amplified click of a camera shutter in tandem with the image of Lecter facing us/Pazzi with a camera to his eye and a mocking smile on his face. The modality (truth-claim) of this moment is elevated beyond the naturalistic by the shocking noise of the camera, into what van Leeuwen calls a sensory modality (1999), where the credibility of the text rests on its ability to provoke emotion rather than its claim to a 'realistic' representation of the world. This is, of course, an appropriate strategy for a text within a genre whose general function is to create an affective response – the only genre named after an affect, 'horror', as the philosopher of film Noel Carroll notes (Carroll, 1990).

Set against this proximity of the audience to the victim, both visually and affectively, are other structures which invite us into closer proximity to Lecter. Intertextually, we have experience of his history across two films – we are more intimately acquainted with him, as it were. This allows us to recognize two features of his murder of Pazzi – firstly that it is satisfyingly elaborate, like the murder of the prison guards in *Silence of the Lambs*; and secondly, that, like all his crimes, it is an act of self-defence, since he is being pursued.

Chris engages with these structures in specific ways. His first clause, like the film, expresses a proximity to Pazzi, who is the subject of his clause just as he is the subject of the film sequence. He inserts himself and the general spectator into the suspense structure of the narrative: 'in your mind you're worried about the detective'. He evaluates Hannibal in various ways which suggest an admiration for the character in keeping with sub-genres of horror which produce likeable monsters as a franchise (Freddy Krueger, in the *Nightmare on Elm Street* series, is another obvious example). He locates himself in relation to the characters, in complex, mobile ways: he seems closer to the detective, Pazzi, at the moment when he imagines him as a victim; but closer to Hannibal in his admiration for him, expressed partly in the most elementary resource language has for representation: naming. Hannibal is named; Pazzi remains anonymous, as 'the detective'.

Secondly, because it is externally produced as speech, Chris's account must be oriented towards its new audience in the world. One aspect of it is clearly determined by us, the researchers who are asking the questions in the interview. It is true that we have simply asked: 'What is the bit you liked best?'

which does not appear at first sight to require anything other than an anecdotal account. However, the fact that the researchers come from a university, that the interview is taking place in the sixth-form college where Chris is an A level student, and that the other two interviewees are fellow A level Media and Film Studies students, all make a difference. So some elements of Chris's account are the A level student talking, as it were: '. . . shows a contrast. . . where you see the difference of character'. This is clearly not the language register he would use with friends after viewing the film.

Other parts of his account, however, do seem to be orientated towards the social situation of the initial viewing with his friends. Here, there is an emphasis on the violent events of the narrative, amplified by the use of gesture, which may be closer to the excited and dramatic talk typical of spectators coming out of a cinema after a film. Such an emphasis is close to the affective core of the film, where the appeal lies in the tradition of slasher horror films. At this core is Chris's focus on the monster Hannibal, whom he regards with a kind of admiring affection.

One of Chris's reasons for liking the sequence is his enjoyment of the teasing nature of the suspense in the sequence, in which Hannibal could act at any moment, but chooses to hold back. This enjoyment, again, is not orientated towards the 'academic' audience, but towards a different social situation, much closer to that in which he enjoyed the film with his mates; and the linguistic register he uses here strongly suggests this social context:

'. . . in the back of your mind you're worried about the detective, whether he's gonna kill him, he could've so easily killed him and had him for breakfast.'

This produces two ideas of narrative: the idea of suspense which is characteristic of the horror film, and the idea of narrative alternatives – what might happen at this point rather than what does happen. At the same time, it represents the general spectator of the horror movie, as *you*: 'in the back of your mind you're worried'.

It orientates itself, as we have seen, towards the social situation of the original viewing with his friends; so that, effectively, we are invited to locate ourselves in this way, rather than, say, as teachers.

Conclusion

In summary, then, we can say that this is a complex, hybrid production of an engagement with a film. It uses the resources of language and gesture to remake narrative images and structures, to evaluate, and to establish different degrees of social proximity, indicating different interpretative communities and his relation to them. Clearly, also, the more abstract interpretative structures he constructs (the suspense mechanism and the contrast between the two aspects of Hannibal) are related to his orientation to both social situations. In other words, we cannot say that watching the film with his friends produces a 'simpler' narrative representation, while thinking of the academic context of sixth form and researchers produces the more abstract interpretation. His awareness of complex characterization and suspense shifts between linguistic registers associated with different social situations.

Chris's interpretative strategies register the different cultural experience (or cultural capital, as Bourdieu would say) of popular cinematic experience as well as the more formal analytical procedures of A level Media Studies. However, his choice of linguistic register is more determined by the orientation of his talk to different intepretive communities than to the ideas he is expressing. This suggests more mobile kinds of engagement than the heavily determined categories of Bourdieu's stratification of cinematic taste imply.

Methodological points

1. Recording interviews. We always record interviews on video. The main reason for this is to record not only voice, but facial expression, gesture and other relevant features of the social situation of the interview, such as who is sitting where, in relation to whom, in what kind of chair, in what kind of room, and so on.

2. Transcribing the interview. Transcripts should show as accurately as possible the words and sounds produced. Hesitations, laughter, overlaps and pauses are all important. Gestures should be described. It is possible to go much further, and notate the rhythmic features of spoken language, as well as the use of tone as a signifying resource. For an account of this, we recommend Halliday (1989).

3. Choosing interviewees. Researchers will have their own criteria for choosing a sample, which may want to represent gendered responses to film, for instance, or a range of ethnic or socio-economic backgrounds. In small studies, like the one in this chapter, the sample group may be opportunistic – the group that happens to be available to the small-scale researcher (a situation typical of teacher-researchers, for whom the obvious opportunistic sample group is their own class).

4. How many in an interview? There were three students in this interview. Having a small group allows the interview to become more of a conversation, with the kinds of interchange that might naturally occur between members of a peer group. In an individual interview, by contrast, the only audience for the interviewee is the researcher, which makes this a much less natural exchange, and raises the problem of the respondent trying to please the interviewer. This, of course, must be weighed against the possibility of the interviewees in a group saying only what will please the peer group. In our experience, the latter possibility is much less of a problem than the former.

6

Key Principles and Practices

We will finish by revisiting some points of practice and principle for researchers working in this field, as well as outlining some areas we have not been able to cover in the space of this book.

Discourse

Discourse is a problematic category and hard to pin down. An advantage of multimodal analysis is that it has ways of paying close attention to detailed aspects of signification; but it is often hard to be as detailed when discussing discursive constructions of a major area of human experience, such as childhood or war. Our approach to this is to try to find semiotic data from the whole context in which the text is being studied, whether this is the making of the text, or its reception and interpretation. So in Chapter 2, while the idea of a discourse of generational conflict is vague and abstract, it becomes specific and concrete once we look at how a group of skateboarders battle for territory with an elderly man from a university building.

We can also look for intertextual clues. Every sign in a text is part of a discourse; but a discourse is necessarily bigger than a single text. When we compared the use of animated cocoa-beans in the chocolate websites analysed in Chapter 3 to similar animations in advertisements for children's cereals, we were looking for a specific signifier employed in a particular discourse associating childhood with 'fun'.

Finally, we can interview makers and readers of texts to find out how the text connects with their views, beliefs and perceptions of the world. This helps to move the idea of text and discourse from their traditional abstract context to a concrete context which is always material. An article by Burn and Reed (1999) analyses a short piece of video by four girls; but also analyses interview transcripts and pieces of writing by the girls. In effect, this is a kind of triangulation as far as research method is concerned – we are exploring the question through the use of three different kinds of data, which is a way to address the question of the validity in the research method.

Processes of design and production

As we mentioned in Chapter 1, a value of multimodality theory is that it regards a text as a process, as unfinished business, rather than as a neat, sealed object on a shelf, or in a timeless space. This means that the whole business of designing and producing a text is of interest, as each stage involves a transformation, adaptation and reworking of the semiotic material available. Each transformation adds another layer, leaves another trace. Each move in the process uses tools of inscription, maybe different tools at each stage, all with their own possibilities and constraints. This has never been more true than it is today of digital media, where the appropriation, transformation and synthesis of earlier signs is, perhaps, the defining characteristic of the medium.

Practical consequences of all this are that researchers need to be alert to all the stages of text-making, collecting draft designs, storyboards, plans, even successive digital versions of a text in its making. As we said about computer game sessions (in which text-reading becomes hard to tell from text-writing), using screen-capture software can be useful here to track what the author is doing.

Alternatively, the researcher can film the processes of text production. While such a video must be regarded as, in some sense, the researcher's construction of events rather than a 'true' record, it can help to produce a more robust, multi-perspectival analysis of the processes of design and production. Also, of course, it provides multimodal information – not only the planning materials and tools, but the talk, action, gesture, location and bodily work of production.

Interpretation

In Chapter 4, we looked at how one teenage spectator interpreted *Hannibal*. We saw that his account was a trans-formation and reconstitution of ideational aspects of the text, as well as an engagement with orientational aspects of the film. We were looking mainly at his use of language and ges-ture, since these were the appropriate and available communi-cative modes for this occasion. It is worth considering how many other kinds of evidence of interpretative work can be explored in research and in what locations. This can range from the excited talk of viewers emerging from a cinema to pieces of writing, drawing and video production made in classrooms.

A further rich seam of textual interpretation is available in the work of fans of particular texts and genres, especially in online fan cultures, where transformations of cult texts become extensive regimes of production in their own right. These appropriations and transformations of texts by fans who Henry Jenkins has called 'textual poachers' (Jenkins, 1992) constitute discursive networks in which researchers can explore questions of fan identity, cultural taste and allegiance, and pleasure, as well as wider conceptions of literacy. Educators are beginning to be interested, for example, in the kinds of narrative writing made by fans of computer games (McClay, 2002). At this point, of course, the question of whether we are dealing with textual reception or production becomes interestingly problematic, a fruitful theoretical route for researchers to pursue.

Questions we have not addressed

The length of this book only permits brief examples of what is possible using a multimodal approach to textual analysis. We will finish by briefly sketching some topics which we have not been able to cover in depth.

Literacies and pedagogies

We have referred briefly to the question of literacy in Chapter 1. All education systems are concerned with literacy. Conventionally, this is restricted to models of print literacy (reading and writing) and associated cultural competences, such as a knowledge of the country's canonical literature. A multimodal view of textuality raises the issue of how the notion of 'literacy' might be expanded to encompass all modes of signification, so that we can think of multiple literacies. In recent years, this has become a somewhat confused debate. Problems include the word literacy and its associations primarily with language – the use of the word 'literacy' to mean both the ability to understand and produce text and to be culturally competent in a wider and vaguer sense – and the more recent use of the term 'digital literacy', suggesting communicative competences specific to digital media. Furthermore, the use of the term 'media literacy' complicates the picture further. In many countries, this means simply the ability to read mass media texts critically. Within education, however, its use is more complex, referring to the ability both to analyse and produce media texts, and accommodating a more positive view of popular cultural texts than the narrower use of 'media literacy' (see the bfi report

Mapping Media Literacy for a recent account of this in the UK).

Many of these uses are strategic rather than analytical, related to policy contexts rather than research contexts. Researchers will need to weigh this in their approach to the idea of 'multimodal literacy'. The central question, perhaps, for researchers to consider is that literacy is to do with learning and teaching – how children acquire the necessary skills or knowledge to understand and make texts in different combinations of modes and media. These processes are, of course, important ones for education researchers to analyse, and it may be that analogies with the learning of print literacy are useful to pursue. For instance, the teaching of print literacy raises the question of metacognitive understanding – the extent to which children can become consciously aware of the processes of communication they engage in – and the value of such understanding.

We have not looked specifically at teaching and learning processes here, though obviously they can form the central focus for education researchers. The exception, perhaps, is in Chapter 3, where we looked at the kinds of learning opportunity offered by the two chocolate websites.

The idea of multimodal pedagogies is deeply problematic for traditional models of the curriculum and the specialist teaching skills which are constructed to serve it. In a study of the multimodal nature of a primary school animation project, we have suggested that the success of this project depended partly upon the teachers involved overcoming traditional subject boundaries, so that Art, Media, English and Music specialists worked together to provide what, for the children, was an integrated multimodal experience (Burn and Parker, 2003). Questions researchers might explore here might include: how different modes and media are used as part of the teaching and learning process; how different modes and media are used to design and produce texts; how the use of these modes and media are taught and learned; and how the pedagogy recognizes and incorporates the discursive contexts of the texts being studied or made.

Distribution

In Chapter 1, we outlined Kress and van Leeuwen's four strata of multimodal communication. Though we have looked at discourse, design and production in the examples in this book, we have not explored distribution. Researchers might want to look at how the media of distribution themselves change the meanings of texts. In Chapter 2, for example, we could have extended our analysis of the skateboarding video to the circumstances of its distribution. It was screened in two contexts not normally available to school media productions. Firstly, as part of a school-produced weekly half-hour programme on a local cable TV station and secondly, at a local arts cinema. In each of these circumstances, new questions would arise for the researcher: who was involved in these further transformations of the text; what signifying properties the different screens of television and cinema contributed; what kinds of audience would be assembled by each medium of distribution; and what new discursive contexts would be constituted?

Distribution is an important issue for education. Media and multimedia texts made by students have traditionally suffered from highly restricted distribution. Regarded as forms of simulation or apprentice exercise, they have often been denied the kinds of distribution to an audience that, in the real world, is usually the whole point of making a text in the first place. The arrival of digital media, especially the internet, provides more opportunities for publication and distribution, though it also changes the social nature of that distribution and of the audiences it reaches.

Analysing texts: units of analysis

Because multimodal analysis yields rich material from very brief segments of text, it is often difficult to know how much or how little to analyse, or what the unit of analysis should be. In these chapters, we have analysed a sequence of film which lasts less than a minute, two or three pages from two websites, a very brief sequence from a videogame and an extract of interview of about one minute. However, we have also referred more generally to the whole text. There is no simple answer to this problem – the analysis needs to be detailed to be really interesting, but it also needs to not lose sight of the structures and contexts within which the fragment of text is meaningful.

The unit of analysis is a different problem. It really depends on what is being analysed. Van Leeuwen's analysis of rhythm in film (1985), for instance, makes rhythmic units across speech, editing and music his focus – so he needs to look at the smallest elements of such structures (the metrical foot of spoken English) as well as the smallest unit of the largest mode included (the shot structure of film editing). In practice, this could mean no more than a few seconds of film, though he looks at rather more than this.

A related problem is how to tabulate and notate the modes in play in a text. In the example above, van Leeuwen uses a kind of timeline which records the words of the film dialogue, the notes of the music track (in conventional musical notation) and the events of the visual track (in words), along with indications of cuts between shots.

In our analysis of the primary school animation referred to above, we have represented the shots by screen grabs (as in Chapter 1 of this book) and aligned these with a description of the music track in words and a record of the dialogue. This notation shows clearly how segments of music, speech and moving image are articulated. It omits other interesting information, however, such as the tonal contours of the children's voices and the harmonic structure of the music.

Endpiece

In all of this, it is important for researchers using a multimodal approach to bear in mind that it is a new and evolving theory. If some methods, terms and techniques are not fixed, then that is to be expected and is, in any case, in accordance with a multimodal view of signification, which sees communication as mobile, versatile and subject to constant change. One of the exciting things about adopting it as an analytical method is the likelihood that, faced with a problem to which the theory has, as yet, no answer, the researcher must extend the theory. In many ways, like any theoretical framework, it should always refuse to become an orthodoxy.

References

Beavis, C. (2001) 'Digital culture, digital literacies: Expanding the notions of text', in Beavis, C. and Durrant, C. (eds) *P(ICT)ures of English: Teachers, Learners and Technology*, pp. 145–61, Wakefield Press, Adelaide

Bigum, C., Lankshear, C., Morgan, W. and Snyder, I. (1997), *Digital Rhetorics: Literacies and Technologies in Education – Current Practices and Future Directions*, Queensland University

Borah, R. (2003) 'Apprentice wizards welcome: Fan communities and the culture of Harry Potter' in Whited, L. (ed.) *The Ivory Tower and Harry Potter: Perspectives on a Literary Phenomenon*, University of Missouri Press

Bordwell, D. and Thompson, K. (2001) *Film Art: an Introduction* (6th edition), New York: McGraw-Hill

Bourdieu, P. (1987) *Distinction: A Social Critique of the Judgment of Taste*, Harvard University Press

Buckingham, D. (1996) *Moving Images: Understanding Children's Emotional Responses to Television*, Manchester: Manchester University Press

Buckingham, D. (2000) *After the Death of Childhood: Growing Up in the Age of Electronic Media*, London: Polity

Buckingham, D. (2002) *Small Screens: Television for Children*, Leicester: Leicester University Press

Buckingham, D. and Sefton-Green, J. (1994) *Cultural Studies Goes to School: Reading and Teaching Popular Media*, London: Taylor and Francis

Buckingham, D., Grahame, J. and Sefton-Green, J. (1995) *Making Media – Practical Production in Media Education*, London: English and Media Centre

Burn, A. and Parker, D. (2001) 'Making your mark: Digital inscription, animation, and a new visual semiotic', *Education, Communication & Information*, Vol. 1, No. 2

Burn, A. and Parker, D. (2003) 'Tiger's Big Plan: Multimodality and the moving image' in Jewitt, C. and Kress, G. (eds) *Multimodal Literacy*, New York: Peter Lang

Burn, A., Brindley, S., Reid, M. *et al.* (2001) 'The Rush of Images: A research report on a study of digital editing and the moving image', *English in Education*, Vol. 35, No. 2, Summer 2001

Burn, A. and Reed, K. (1999b) 'Digiteens: Media literacies and digital technologies in the secondary classroom', *English in Education*, 33:3

Carroll, N. (1990), *The Philosophy of Horror: Or, Paradoxes of the Heart*, New York: Routledge

Clover, C. (1993), *Men, Women and Chainsaws*, London: BFI

Eisenstein, S.M. (1968) *The Film Sense*, trans. J. Layda, London: Faber and Faber

Genette, G. (1980) *Narrative Discourse*, Oxford: Blackwell

Goffman, E. (1959) *The Presentation of Self in Everyday Life*, New York: Anchor Books

Hodge, R. and Kress, K. (1988) *Social Semiotics*, Cambridge: Polity

Kress, K. and van Leeuwen, T. (1996) *Reading Images: The Grammar of Visual Design*, London: Routledge

Halliday, M.A.K. (1974) *Explorations in the Functions of Language*, London: Arnold

Halliday, M.A.K. (1985) *An Introduction to Functional Grammar*, London: Arnold

Halliday, M.A.K. (1989) *Spoken and Written Language*, Oxford: Oxford University Press

Jenkins, H. (1992) *Textual Poachers: Television Fans and Participatory Culture*, New York: Routledge

Jewitt, C. and Kress, G. (eds) (2003) *Multimodal Literacy*, New York: Peter Lang

Kress, G., Jewitt, C., Tsatsarelis, C. and Ogborn, J. (2001) *Multimodality Teaching and Learning: The Rhetorics of the Science Classroom*, London: Continuum

Kress, G. and van Leeuwen, T. (2000) *Multimodal Discourse: The Modes and Media of Contemporary Communication*, London: Arnold

Lanham, R. (2001) 'What's Next for Text?' *Education, Communication and Information*, Vol.1, No. 1

Laurel, B. (1993) *Computers as Theatre*, Reading, MA: Addison-Wesley

Lave, J., and Wenger, E. (1991) *Situated Learning : Legitimate Peripheral Participation*, Cambridge: Cambridge University Press

Lemke, J. (2002) 'Travels in Hypermodality', *Visual Communication* 1(3): 299–325

Mackereth, M. and Anderson, J. (2000) 'Computers, video games, and literacy: What do girls think?' *The Australian Journal of Language and Literacy* 23(3): 184–95

McClay, J. (2002) 'Hidden "Treasure": New genres, new media and the teaching of writing', *English in Education*, Vol. 36, No. 1, 46–55

Metz, C. (1974) *Film Language*, Chicago, IL: Chicago University Press

Murray, J. (1998) *Hamlet on the Holodeck*, Cambridge, MA: MIT Press

Ong, W. (2002) *Orality and Literacy: The Technologizing of the Word*, London: Routledge

Orr Vered, K. (1998) 'Blue group boys play *Incredible Machine*, Girls play hopscotch: Social discourse and gendered play at the computer', in Sefton-Green, J. (ed.) *Digital Diversions: Youth Culture in the Age of Multimedia*. London: UCL Press

Parker, D. and Sefton-Green, J. (2000) *Edit-Play*, London: BFI

Poole, S. (2000) *Trigger Happy : Videogames and the Entertainment Revolution*, New York: Arcade

Raney, K. (1997) *Visual Literacy: Issues and Debates*, Middlesex University

Schott, G. and Horrell, K. (2000) 'Girl Gamers and their Relationship with the Gaming Culture', *Convergence*, 6(4), 36–53.

Sefton-Green, J. (1999) 'Media Education, but not as we know it: Digital Technology and the end of Media Studies', *The English & Media Magazine* No. 40, Summer 1999

Sinker, R. (2000) 'Making Multimedia', in Sefton-Green, J. and Sinker, R. (eds), *Evaluating Creativity*, London: Routledge

Tudor, A. (1999) *Decoding Culture*, London: Sage

van Leeuwen, T. (1985) 'Rhythmic structure of the film text', in van Dijk (ed.), *Discourse and Communication*, Berlin: de Gruyter

van Leeuwen, T. (1999) *Speech, Music, Sound*, London: Macmillan

Index